NO
OTHER
GOSPEL!

Other Fortress Press books by Carl E. Braaten

*Justification: The Article by which the Church
Stands or Falls*

*Our Naming of God: Problems and Prospects of
God-Talk Today,* editor

The Theology of Wolfhart Pannenberg,
edited with Philip Clayton (Augsburg)

*The So-Called Historical Jesus and
the Historic, Biblical Christ,* translator and editor

*The Apostolic Imperative: Nature and Aim of
the Church's Mission and Ministry* (Augsburg)

Christian Dogmatics, edited
with Robert Jenson, 2 vols.

Principles of Lutheran Theology

No Other Gospel!

*Christianity among the
World's Religions*

Carl E. Braaten

FORTRESS PRESS
Minneapolis

NO OTHER GOSPEL!
Christianity among the World's Religions

Copyright © 1992 Augsburg Fortress. All rights reserved. Except for brief quotations in critical articles or reviews, no part of this book may be reproduced in any manner without prior written permission from the publisher. Write to: Permissions, Augsburg Fortress, 426 S. Fifth St., Box 1209, Minneapolis, MN 55440.

Scripture quotations, unless otherwise noted, are from the New Revised Standard Version Bible, copyright © 1989, by the Division of Christian Education of the National Council of the Churches of Christ in the United States of America.

Library of Congress Cataloging-in-Publication Data

Braaten, Carl E., 1929–
    No other gospel! : Christianity among the world's religions / Carl
E. Braaten.
        p.   cm.
    Includes bibliographical references and index.
    ISBN 0-8006-2539-0 (alk. paper)
    1. Christianity and other religions.   2. Religious pluralism—
-Christianity.   3. Christianity—Essence, genius, nature.   4. Jesus
Christ—Person and offices.   I. Title.
    BR127.B66   1992
    261.2—dc20   91-35747
                                                                        CIP

The paper used in this publication meets the minimum requirements of American National Standard for Information Sciences—Permanence of Paper for Printed Library Materials, ANSI Z329.48-1984. ∞™

Manufactured in the U.S.A.   AF 1-2539
96   95   94   2   3   4   5   6   7   8   9   10

To my graduate students at
Lutheran School of Theology at Chicago

Contents

Acknowledgments

THE CONTENTS OF THIS BOOK have evolved over the past five years in response to the challenge posed by current radical theologies of religious pluralism. Chapter 1 originally appeared in German in *Kerygma und Dogma* 36, Jahrgang, 1990/1, Januar/ März, 56–71 as "*Gott und das Evangelium: Pluralismus und Apostasie in der amerikanischen Theologie*" and is reprinted by permission. Chapter 2 originally appeared in *Interpretation,* vol. 40, (October 1986), pp. 341–53 as "The Problem of the Absoluteness of Christianity" and is reprinted by permission. Chapter 3 is original to this volume. Chapter 4 was originally given as a paper entitled "A Lutheran Theology of Religious Pluralism" at a seminar sponsored by the Lutheran World Federation Commission on Studies, and is included in a volume published as *Lutheran World Federation Report* 23/24, 1988. It is reprinted by permission. A part of chapter 5, reprinted by permission, originally appeared as "Preaching Christ in an Age of Religious Pluralism" in *Word and World* 9.3, 1989. Chapter 6 was a paper, "The Triune God: The Source and Model of Christian Unity and Mission," read at the American Society of Missiology and originally appeared in *Missiology: An International Review* 18.4 (October 1990) and is reprinted by permission. Chapter 7 was a lecture delivered at the Martin Luther Colloquium 1989 and originally appeared as "God in Public Life: A Rehabilitation of the Lutheran Idea of the 'Orders of Creation,' " in *Encounter with Luther,* vol. 4, and is reprinted by permission. A revised version of "God in Public Life" appeared in *First Things* 8 (December 1990) and is also reprinted by permission.

NO
OTHER
GOSPEL!

Introduction:
Question Mark–
Exclamation Point

PAUL F. KNITTER HAS WRITTEN a landmark book on Christianity and the world religions that bears the title *No Other Name?*[1] The reason for the question mark is to call into question the traditional biblical-Christian claim that Jesus Christ is unique, normative, decisive, and final as the self-revelation of God and the salvation of the world. Acts 4:12 declares: "There is salvation in no one else, for there is no other name under heaven given among mortals by which we must be saved." In stark contrast, this book bears the title *No Other Gospel!* The exclamation point, however, is included in the title for a reason similar to Knitter's. I can find no better way to accentuate Paul's emphasis in Gal 1:6-9, where again and again he warns his readers about turning to a "different gospel": "a gospel contrary to what we proclaimed to you"; but he also says, "not that there is another gospel." In 2 Cor 11:1-6, Paul refers to some unnamed "super-apostles" who arrived proclaiming "another Jesus" and "a different gospel," not the gospel of God that Paul preached at Corinth.

Today we stand once again between the question mark imposed by the skeptical spirit of our age and the exclamation point punctuating the christological kerygma of apostolic times. Perhaps many of us live simultaneously with both the question mark and the exclamation point, moving back and forth in a rhythm of doubt and faith. The question mark without the exclamation point may lead to self-aggrandizing skepticism. We may become too dogmatic about our questioning spirit and

1

apotheosize the unbelief of our postmodern age. The exclamation point without the question mark may lead to the spirit of fanaticism in which the assurances of apostolic faith are frozen in a system of absolutes ideologically immunized against the changes of time and history. Both the mark and the point are ingredients in a faith seeking understanding.

In a deeper sense, however, the exclamation point in the title of this book punctuates not my assertion but the apostle's. Every theologian must decide whether to reiterate the apostle's declaration or to confront it with a question mark. I argue in this book that the theologian's decision to prefer one punctuation mark over the other is a decision for or against the gospel itself. My preference is to put a big question mark to the pluralist position that holds either that the exclusive claim of the gospel can be attributed to the outdated cultural situation in which New Testament Christianity originated, or that we can maintain continuity with the identity and substance of the Christian faith without it, or that it can be written off as mere hyperbole of the heart.

The exclusive claim of the gospel has been dismissed as "the myth of Christian uniqueness" by the pluralistic theology of religions.[2] We owe this theology a debt of gratitude for raising the most urgent questions facing the church in its theology and mission. When it comes to essentials, the old questions are not that different from the new. How can it be that there is no other name, no other gospel? The ancient Gnostics asked the same question and so do the modern ones. Are there not many revealers of God, many saviors of humanity? The primitive church encountered these questions, and so do contemporary Christians in dialogue with other religions. Is not the claim that Jesus is unique a myth that moderns have outgrown? Are there not many ways of salvation, as many as there are religions in the world?

In the attempt to answer these questions, Christian theology is today teetering on the brink of suicidal confusion. This book aims to make clear what we as the contemporary heirs of the Reformation believe about the uniqueness and universality of the gospel of Jesus Christ. We are Christian believers, and we do not enter the dialogue with other religions with empty hearts and vacant minds. We are evangelical catholics standing in the

Lutheran confessional tradition, and we hold certain truths to be solidly based on divine revelation attested by Holy Scripture. We propose four dogmatic propositions to which all Christians ought to subscribe if they are faithful to God's revelation in Jesus Christ: First, Jesus Christ is the personal event in whom God's final revelation has already occurred, so that we do not "wait for another" (Matt 11:3). Second, faith in Jesus as the Christ means real personal participation in God's eschatological salvation. Third, the church is the community of believers who must proclaim Jesus of Nazareth as the sole Savior of humankind until God's kingdom arrives in its final glory. Fourth, God's will is that all shall be saved and that the whole creation, now in a struggle for life, will at last reach its fulfilling future in the reign of God through Jesus Christ our Lord.

The systematic theological problem that devolves upon us is how to conceive the attainment of the universal goal of salvation by means of God's particular revelation in Jesus of Nazareth. In the history of Christian theology, there has always been a fight between the particularists and the universalists.

The particularists have classically stressed the pole of historical contingency. They point to a double contingency: first, the historical event of Jesus Christ, and second, the existential experience of faith in him as personal Lord and Savior. If we hold unqualifiedly to these concrete conditions of salvation, the vast majority of people in the world—past, present, and future— would obviously be excluded by sheer historical contingency. The particular means of salvation then appear inadequate to the task of realizing God's universal goal of salvation, and the Christian mission becomes something like salvaging human cargo from a ship headed for eternal disaster. Only a few make it into the ark of salvation; all the rest perish in the flood.

To the universalists, such a pessimistic outcome is morally repugnant because the content of the gospel is universal in scope. The "one and only" statements of the New Testament to which the particularists point can be matched by the cosmic "all things" *(ta panta)* statements that ring out with the hope of universal salvation through Christ. One example appears in Eph 1:8-10: "With all wisdom and insight he has made known to us the mystery of his will, according to his good pleasure that he set forth in Christ, as a plan for the fullness of time, to gather up all things in him, things in heaven and things on earth." Here is the biblical base for what is called an eschatologial panentheism (not pantheism).

I am committed to a theology that moves within the field of tension marked by both the particularist and universalist aspects of the biblical vision of the eschatological consummation. The particularist affirms the basic Christian belief that salvation has already arrived in Jesus Christ and through personal participation in his self-embodying community. As a rule, however, the particularist surrenders the hope of a final restitution of all things in Christ (Eph 1:10). Various types of particularism range from the Calvinist doctrine of double predestination to the Arminian doctrine of free will and moral responsibility. The particularist begins in monism (the whole creation comes from the one God) but ends in a radical dualism (the whole creation becomes eternally divided, with a small remnant getting to heaven and all the rest going to hell). The price that particularism pays, however, is the rationalization of only one side of biblical eschatology.

The universalist dreams that all things culminate in God's everlasting reign of freedom and fulfillment. God's intention that all shall be saved will not miscarry. The fragmented condition of humanity in history will ultimately be resolved into the unity of eternal life, when God will be all in all. The universal vision has been projected in two different opposing ways: Humanistic universalism in the deistic or unitarian line denies the chief articles of the Christian faith concerning human bondage to sin and death as well as the divine act of redemption in the person and work of Jesus Christ. In contrast, christocentric universalism extrapolates to the future from the biblical history of salvation and perceives that God's omnipotent love will somehow be victorious in the end, in spite of all destructive and demonic forces at work to the contrary.

The tension between the historical particularity of Christian faith and its eschatological universality has been resolved in, or perhaps dissolved into, a number of contemporary theories of the relation of Christianity to other religions. I will deal with them in various chapters of this book. Two of the most imaginative are those by Karl Rahner and Karl Barth. Karl Rahner has constructed his theory on the basis of the ancient patristic doctrine of the universal Logos. The idea of Logos was the magic key the early Christian apologists used to explain how all people have access to the experience and knowledge of truth, beauty, and goodness. Karl Rahner coined the phrase "anonymous Christians"[3] for those who participate in the divine grace and salvation through the presence of the universal Logos in religious and moral systems other than Christian.

Karl Barth grounded his universal vision not in the universal Logos at work above and beyond the incarnation but in God's election of all humanity in Jesus Christ. The rejection and the election of all persons occur in Christ. Jesus Christ is the only person who is really rejected, the only reprobate human. No one is rejected apart from Jesus Christ. The rejection of Jesus Christ on the cross takes up the rejection of all people so that they can participate fully also in his election. This is a universalism of grace that has no room for merit. Unlike Rahner, Barth does not believe that people receive salvation through the rituals and ceremonies of their own religions. Religions as such are not ways of salvation.

Karl Barth's doctrine is attractive, and readers of this book as well as of other writings of mine will observe that I also work with a strong emphasis on the centrality of Christ. I share with Barth what I call a christocentric trinitarian monotheism, but I have to confess that as a Lutheran theologian I cannot be a good Barthian. A chief difficulty is the way Barth places the election of Christ for all people into a prehistory, into the eternal preexistence of the God-man. Perhaps because of his Calvinist tradition, he seems to locate the process of redemption outside the sphere of history, in a time before all time. The ahistorical character of this doctrine of election is due to a defective eschatology, an eschatology that suffers from an allergy to time and history. Such an eschatology can hardly motivate the universal Christian mission within the horizon of the world's religions, which explains why the Barthian school of theology has not moved to the frontiers of interreligious encounter in mission and dialogue.

The point of view that characterizes this work has been shaped by three distinct but related movements in theology. The first is the Lutheran principle of justification by grace alone, through faith alone, on account of Christ alone *(sola gratia, per fidem, propter Christum*).[4] The second is the eschatological theme highlighted in the sixties by the theologians of hope. For some, this theme turned out to be a passing fad; but I believe it is still usable theological currency backed by the gold of the gospel itself.[5] The third is the new trinitarian doctrine of God, which overcomes the dualistic thinking that separates God's eternal being from God's self-revelation in and through history. Karl Rahner's rule is decisive for all the new trinitarians: "The 'economic' Trinity is the 'immanent' Trinity and the 'immanent' Trinity is the 'economic' Trinity."[6] These formative principles for a Christian theology of the gospel that defines the place of Christianity among world religions require further attention.

Paul Knitter correctly sees that theologians who operate with the principle of justification in fidelity to the Reformation tradition are so committed to the fundamental belief in salvation through Christ alone that they cannot affirm all religions as equal ways of salvation. These theologians see Jesus Christ as the one and only Savior of the world because, as Knitter writes, "they are dealing with the *articulus stantis et cadentis ecclesiae,* the article (of faith) on which the church stands or falls. To jeopardize belief in the salvific centrality of Christ is to tear the heart out of Christianity."[7] The principle of justification holds that every interpretation of religion as personal experience or of the religions as ritual systems of communal experience must be a corollary of God's way of redeeming the world and justifying sinners through Jesus Christ. If the principle of justification (what Paul Tillich called "the Protestant principle") does not function in this critical way, it is good for nothing and has yielded to some other norm. Since religions share in the universal human condition of sin and rebellion, they cannot serve victoriously as a means of deliverance. They are mired in human bondage and cannot save themselves or anyone else. The word of final hope comes indeed to religion and not through religion. This critical relativizing word of justification applies to Christianity as much as to any other religion because Christianity often presents itself as salvation and thus nullifies the necessity of Christ's death and resurrection.

Eschatology is also fundamental to the theology of the religions, and it points to the future when "people will come from east and west, from north and south, and will eat in the kingdom of God" (Luke 13:29). Jesus of Nazareth actualized the kingdom of God in his own ministry of life, death, and resurrection. When the first missionaries preached the gospel of Jesus Christ to the nations, they announced that that was the goal to which God has been leading them all along. The God who comes in Christ has been hiddenly present to all epochs prior to Christ as the power of their end, both in the sense of judgment and of fulfillment. The eschatological light of God's coming kingdom, which shines in Christ, flashes back upon all the religions as the end to which God has been directing them unawares. They may all appear retroactively to have witnessed the coming of the fullness of truth beyond their own provisional and limited knowledge of God. The eschatological kingdom that becomes really present in Jesus is the dynamic of the apostolic mission whose essential purpose is to announce the comprehensive universality of salvation for all people, no matter when or wherever they may exist. The eschatological validity of God's saving power in Jesus' history could not be maintained as the subject matter of the universal mission of the gospel if he did not mediate the comprehensive future of all people, no matter what their religious background. No Christian group has ever existed that did not originally come from some other religious tradition prior to conversion and baptism. Nobody can be born a Christian; faith is not a natural human state into which one can enter by birth. If there were some other future than the future of God in Christ to which the religions are pointing, then that other future would prove to be the sovereign of the universe and maker of heaven and earth. Our eschatology must be consistent with the First Commandment: "You shall have no other gods before me."

The significance of the doctrine of the Trinity for Christian theology of world religions remains vastly underdeveloped, especially among those who have contributed most to its contemporary renaissance (for example, Karl Barth and Eberhard Jüngel). This lack is being remedied, I believe, with the publication of Wolfhart Pannenberg's *Systematic Theology,* which goes far to join a trinitarian doctrine of God with a universal-historical theology of the world religions. The doctrine of the Trinity begins with Jesus' special relation to the One he called Abba and then takes a long, winding road that leads to Nicaea and Chalcedon. The christocentric trinitarian paradigm is the way of orthodox Christianity to protect itself from the incursion of gnostic and new-age forms of speculation about salvation, which are legion today. Metaphysical claims implied in a trinitarian doctrine of God address the question of the source and scope of revelation and salvation and help us to distinguish one from the other. Theologies of religious pluralism generally conclude that people who possess knowledge of God apart from biblical revelation have no need of Christ. That might be so if there were no proper distinction between revelation and salvation. Not all revelation is saving revelation; nonsalvific revelation of God gives rise to the unending quest for salvation in the religions.

All three streams of thought coincide on the christological issue. We are facing a conflict in Christology as great as the ancient controversies over the three persons of the Godhead (Nicaea) and the two natures of Christ (Chalcedon). The conflict today can be formulated this way: Does Jesus model the salvation that God is working universally through all the religions? Or is what happens in Jesus the sole constitutive cause of the salvation that God delivers to the world? Is the linkage between Jesus and divine salvation loose or tight? Is the linkage so loose that Christology can break away from Christ into some kind of anonymous principle that can be filled with all sorts of religious experiences?[8] When we confess that Jesus is the Christ, or Savior, or God, do we let the unique person of Jesus himself control the meaning of each of the predicates? Or do we fill them first with our own supposedly fulfilling experiences of life and then apply them to Jesus as one among many expressions of the divine-human encounter? Then Jesus becomes merely an outstanding exemplification of what we can already experience and know from other possible sources. The degree to which Jesus exemplifies our spiritual and moral ideals is up to us to say. On the other hand, the new affirmation of a christocentric trinitarian paradigm offers a much more promising resource for thinking about the relation between the gospel, Christianity, and other world religions.

The pluralistic theology of the religions that is in vogue within some academic and ecumenical circles operates with a loose linkage between God and Christ and Jesus. The radical theocentrists want to speak of God without Christ, and the basis and content of their God-language have little or nothing to do with Christ or the gospel. They seem to operate with the rule that the lower the Christology, the better the dialogue. From their perspective, only those who approach the dialogues with other religions with a low Christology are welcome to take a seat in the parliament of the world religions. Orthodox evangelical Christians are not as welcome as new-age Gnostics and Ebionites. Belief in the incarnation is presumably a liability in interreligious dialogue. Where do the theocentric pluralists get their idea of God if not from the salvation historical revelation of God in Christ? If they have some other model or norm for speaking of God, they are proclaiming another gospel.

The trinitarian paradigm for the interreligious dialogues emphasizes that Christocentrism is simply the Christian way of being theocentric. Christ is not a substitute for God, and apart from Christ we are not sure of what we know. At best, a Christless God is a hidden God *(deus absconditus)* whose hind parts *(posteriora Dei)* are indistinguishable from the face of the devil. The underlying Christology of the new theocentrists is most akin to Arianism, whose Christ is of a lower order of being than God. In Arianism, God and Christ mean something ontologically different. In biblical Christian faith, Christocentrism underscores the identity of the God who is really God. If the new theocentrists enter an interreligious dialogue with some other God in mind than the God of the gospel, they should understand that from a Christian perspective they are not saying anything very interesting about God at all.

There is something imperialistic about the argument of the theocentric pluralists such as Paul Knitter and John Hick. They contend that the ones most qualified for the coming interreligious dialogues in this post-Copernican age are those who have removed the scandal of the gospel. Somehow they believe that it is appropriate for Christians to meet faithful Jews, Muslims, Hindus, and Buddhists in dialogue, but only on the condition that they acknowledge that their Christian faith is founded on a mythic incarnation that no modern educated person can believe. My opinion to the contrary is that interreligious dialogue becomes interesting only when we meet, converse, and try to understand and accept each other as persons committed to the core convictions of our respective faiths, without translating the symbols of that core into some supraconfessional philosophy of religion to which no believing community adheres. When we as Christians meet Muslims, Hindus, or Buddhists, we do not accomplish anything if we search for the anonymous Christian in them, if we only appreciate the ways in which they are so much like us, and if we avoid the recalcitrant otherness and strangeness of their belief systems. Why should the dialogues invite only the modernized version of religions whose representatives may be merely a minority of enlightened liberals with scarcely any religious constituency to speak of?

My interest in the theme of Christianity among world religions is partly motivated by a commitment to the mission of the gospel to the nations. For some churches and theologies, the missionary aspect of Christianity has died altogether. For some, the missionary ideal was a mistake from the beginning; the apostles should have stayed in Jerusalem. Such thinking is a negation of New Testament Christianity. The message that the apostles believed and proclaimed concerning Jesus Christ includes the universal mission as part of its essence. The eschatological future of the world that Jesus represented is now verifying its universal validity through the mission to the world. The world is incomplete and its future is still unknown. Only the biblical history of promise anticipates what will become of the world in the end. Those who preach the gospel are wagering while the race is still on that the truth both of the world and of its religions is not manifest in what they already are in themselves, in their own incompleteness.

The gospel declares that Christ is the manifestation of the truth of what all things shall become in their fullness. The power of his and the Father's Spirit is driving the mission of the gospel of God's kingdom. Of utmost importance in this gospel is the element of the comprehensive universality of the kingdom as the salvation of the whole world. The mission operates within the horizon of the challenge that the world has not yet received or accepted the knowledge of its own future in the kingdom of God.

The universality of the truth, which has arrived in Jesus of Nazareth and is now advanced by the mission, is an eschatological reality that exists beyond the frontiers of the church.

The church is not yet universal. Its catholicity is an attribute of the kingdom and therefore of the church, but only insofar as it already is a participation of the eschatological kingdom. The church humbly shows to the other religions that it is also on the way and that it is not the goal itself, which will help to break down the resistance that every finite movement generates in others when it arrogates to itself the position of finality. Only eschatological consciousness in the church can relativize its own self-understanding in face of the absolute truth-claim of the gospel to which it points, just as John the Baptist pointed away from himself to the One who was mightier than he. The church is always weakest when it claims too much for itself. An overstatement of the claim alienates others who should be invited to participate in universal salvation without being put off by a scandalizing church.

The demise of eschatology as the driving power of the mission will always result in ersatz proposals about the church's gospel mission to the nations. In some circles of Western Christianity, the mission has been reduced to a this-worldly potpourri of ecological, economic, social, and political good works that are the proper business of the body politic and its specialized institutions. When churches in Eastern Europe attempted to accredit themselves in their Marxist socialist settings, they became the peace-and-justice propaganda voice of bureaucratic Communism and thus discredited themselves in the eyes of the people who were struggling to overthrow their regimes. The resultant confusion manifested the two ways in which God works in the world: the way of law and the administration of justice on the left hand, and the way of love and the proclamation of the gospel on the right hand. The church must persistently ask: What in the world should the church be doing that the world cannot do for itself? A renewal of the two-kingdoms teaching of Luther can assist the church in drawing the proper distinction between God's twofold revelation and activity without identifying them and also without separating them.

This introduction makes clear that the theme of *No Other Gospel!* takes us into many controversial issues at the forefront of debate in church and theology. The theological position for which I argue cannot claim to be part of an emerging consensus in postmodern theology. My position echoes a minority voice both in the history of Christianity and in theology today; and even though it is not a lone voice, in American theology it holds at best a marginal position in relation to the establishment of mainline liberal Protestantism.

The core conviction advanced in every chapter of this book is the biblical-Christian claim that in Jesus of Nazareth the eschatological truth has appeared once-for-all in a unique event with universal relevance. Christian theology cannot surrender the claim of eschatological finality in connection with the person and work of Jesus Christ. Any attempt to compromise this claim either to accommodate religious pluralism or to promote tolerance and mutual good will yield a different gospel. I do not believe, therefore, that the new pluralistic theology of religions promoted by Paul Knitter and John Hick, which is spreading like wildfire in academic and ecumenical circles, is a genuine way to handle the problem of pluralism, nor does it hold much promise for the longer future.

Pluralism is not an unprecedented problem for the church. The apostolic church encountered pluralism from the beginning by witnessing to Jews, Greeks, Romans, and others in the great melting pot of Hellenistic culture and the Pax Romana. The church was called into existence from out of the many nations, each with its own religious culture. Moreover, pluralism comes into the church itself from the many-splendored creation which God is restoring through his redemptive work in Christ. The church in history is not a monolith. She affirms the many forms of social and cultural life. She affirms the various conditions of life that have to do with sex and age and tribe and language and race and culture and nationality. She invites them all to enter and take part in the kingdom of Christ for the sake of their fulfillment. Pluralism is a positive and necessary dimension of the life of the one, holy, catholic, and apostolic church.

Pluralism is not the enemy of our eschatological faith. Our trinitarian vision of ultimate reality offers a full embrace of our pluralistic world of experience. The history of the church itself gives ample evidence of a plurality of creedal and doctrinal expressions as well as of liturgical, devotional, and artistic expressions. If the church living in history is open both to the future of God's coming kingdom and to the world with its wealth of cultural forms, will she not also be equally open to all the world's religions as ways of salvation on a par with the way of Jesus Christ? The answer to this question will be pursued in the following chapters. Here I need only say that there are limits to pluralism drawn by the gospel itself—definite limits. The apostle Paul warns the church in Rome: "Do not be conformed to this world" (Rom 12:2). He warned against becoming slaves "to the elemental spirits of the world" (Gal 4:3) and against those who would make "you captive through philosophy and empty deceit, according to human tradition" (Col 2:8). Apparently Paul encountered new-age spiritualists in his day too. The church's openness to the world and its future is shaped and defined by the historical particularity of its identity in the gospel. It is possible for a church to become a counterfeit church, a church of the Antichrist, by losing the gospel, closing down the channels of grace, blocking the presence of Christ in Word and sacraments, and secularizing itself into a second-rate imitation of the world. The Christian church lives because of a particular event of history and the traditions it generates by its eschatological force, which in principle is the only norm that limits the pluralism acceptable by the church. The Christian faith has a particular content. It makes a particular claim to truth: the all-fulfilling future of humankind and of the world's salvation has already arrived in Jesus of Nazareth, the Jew of Nazareth. Any church that either ceases to affirm the ultimacy of this event in the history of salvation or attempts to place alongside it other events of equal validity will fall into idolatry and apostasy. Just as the church in the third century could name and refute the heresy of Arianism, and just as the church in the twentieth century struggled against the apostasy of the Nazis' Aryan doctrine, so the church of the twenty-first century will be called upon to escape the deluge of neo-Gnosticism that places Jesus reverently into a pantheon of spiritual heroes.

[1]

American Protestantism
Lacks a Reformation

AFTER HIS LAST TRIP to America in 1939, Dietrich Bonhoeffer wrote an essay that was published only after the war, "Protestantismus ohne Reformation."[1] It was a report of what he had observed firsthand in American Christianity. Among the many things he said, several of the most interesting will serve as a kind of text for my own interpretation of American theology exactly half a century later. Bonhoeffer said: "It has been given to Americans less than any other people in the world to achieve the visible unity of the church of God on earth. It has been given to Americans more than any other people in the world to manifest a pluralism of Christian beliefs and denominations."[2] I will be reflecting on the phenomenon of pluralism in American theology, which I consider to be a sheer fact that can be objectively reported. Further, Bonhoeffer observed: "The rejection of Christology is characteristic of the whole of present-day American theology. Christianity basically amounts to religion and ethics in American theology. Consequently, the person and work of Christ fall into the background and remain basically not understood in this theology."[3] I will also be accounting for this rejection of Christology in American theology, and I admittedly share Bonhoeffer's interpretation. Bonhoeffer concluded his essay with a verdict and a challenge, which are also thematic for my presentation: "God has not given a reformation to American Christianity. . . . The decisive task today is to have a dialogue between American Protestantism without a reformation and the church of the reformation."[4]

Fifty years later this dialogue still remains a task to be accomplished. Bonhoeffer knew that Lutheranism in America has been relatively isolated from the religious mainstream. Its confessional theology has been kept alive in ethnic ghettos remote from the chief centers of theological learning: the divinity schools of Harvard, Yale, and Chicago universities. Only in this generation have Lutheran theologians joined the pluralistic faculties of theology, but they are mostly specialists in some field of religious studies and not systematic theologians; therefore, the heart of the theology of the Reformation—its witness to the God of the gospel—remains marginal in the variety of schools of theology on the American scene. If Bonhoeffer would return to America today, he would have to say déjà vu! He would probably observe that there has still been no reformation of the church and theology in America and that Protestantism still lacks a reformation.

Many had hoped that the beginnings of a reformation of American Protestantism were visibly under way after World War II with the combined influence of the Niebuhr brothers (Reinhold and H. Richard), the Luther renaissance (epitomized by Roland Bainton), the biblical theology of G. Ernest Wright and John Bright, and the enormous popularity of Paul Tillich. A kind of neoorthodoxy was apparently taking root in American soil. The earlier theology of Protestant liberalism and of the Social Gospel Movement was readily dismissed with a few slogans. None was more apropos than H. Richard Niebuhr's characterization of modern Protestantism in America in the following words: "A God without wrath brought men without sin into a kingdom without judgment through the ministrations of a Christ without a cross."[5] Reinhold Niebuhr's Gifford Lectures, *The Nature and Destiny of Man,* seemed to have overcome the liberals' anthropology, which was based on the modern myth of progress, by reviving Luther's realistic understanding of the will's bondage to sin and the seductions of evil. Now the pendulum has swung back, and the ghost of the old liberalism appears within a plurality of so-called postmodern theologies. The coalition that was branded neoorthodoxy is virtually dead— salvific *(Heilsgeschichte)* biblical theology, dialectical theology, Kierkegaardian and Luther studies, and the dogmatics of the various theologians of revelation. We are engulfed in a culture of theological pluralism whose common denominator is exactly what Bonhoeffer observed—a rejection of Christology, a failure to work within a theological paradigm whose flaming center is the definitive revelation of the gospel of God in the person and work of Jesus Christ.

Pluralism in American Theology

David Tracy, professor of theology in the Divinity School of the University of Chicago, has oriented his major theological works around the concept of pluralism in contemporary theology. In three of his books, *Blessed Rage for Order, The Analogical Imagination,* and *Plurality and Ambiguity,* Tracy reflects on the theme of pluralism as the chief characteristic of the present situation. Most theologians seem to fear pluralism as something that erodes authority, dissolves absolutes, and washes away the foundations of faith. For Tracy, however, pluralism is a positive value. It prompts the theologian to reflect on the pluralism that exists in Scripture and the Christian tradition, to be open to a variety of religious experiences, and to learn from different perspectives on our world situation. Pluralism also forces the theologian to think in terms of a plurality of systematic structures, and David Tracy practices the art of entering into conversation with all the trends of the day—in theology, philosophy, literary criticism, and social analysis. Conversation is linked with pluralism; it is the required strategy to keep one's spiritual tradition open to all in our pluralistic setting.

While David Tracy as a theologian greets pluralism as something good, his secular colleague at the University of Chicago, Allan Bloom, professor of philosophy and social thought, reaches quite the opposite conclusion in his *The Closing of the American Mind.* The culture of pluralism has numbed the nerve of true intellectual inquiry, which must presuppose that there is truth and that not all opinions are equal. Bloom begins his book with loathing sarcasm:

> There is one thing a professor can be absolutely certain of: almost every student entering the university believes, or says he believes, that truth is relative. If this belief is put to the test, one can count on the students' reaction: they will be uncomprehending. . . . The students' backgrounds are as various as America can provide. . . .

They are unified only in their relativism and in their allegiance to equality. . . . The relativity of truth is not a theoretical insight but a moral postulate, the condition of a free society, or so they see it. Relativism is necessary to openness, and this is the virtue, the only virtue, which all education has dedicated itself to inculcating. Openness—and the relativism that makes it the only plausible stance in the face of the various claims to truth and various ways of life and kinds of human beings—is the great insight of our times.[6]

Bloom heaps scorn on these traits of the American mind: relativism, pluralism, and openness. Relativism asserts that no one has the right to say that one thing is better than another. The purpose of education is to get students to see that there are no absolutes and to make all students open to a plurality of options on everything from religion and music to politics and sex.

By surveying some of the current trends in American theology, we find that cultural pressures are seemingly irresistible for theologians to worship at the altar of these values in higher education: relativism, pluralism, and openness. We can roughly distinguish three types of theology, each of which itself represents a spectrum of positions.

The first is primarily concerned with the issue of Christian *identity,* which involves faithfulness to Scripture, its revelation and authority, and the creeds and dogmas of the classical tradition. There are both Catholic and evangelical theologians who opt for this strategy.

The second is concerned primarily with the issue of rational *intelligibility,* which reassesses the claims of religion or Christianity on the basis of a commitment to contemporary modes of experience and understanding. A wide variety of positions share this apologetic concern for intelligibility, from those of the older process-theologians such as Schubert Ogden and John Cobb to the newer deconstructionists, such as Mark C. Taylor and Charles E. Winquist, as well as to the new theocentrism, including the theocentric ethics of James Gustafson and the theocentric religious pluralism of Paul Knitter and John Hick. All of these theologians are radical revisionists who fit their conception of Christianity into a contemporary paradigm of values and beliefs, and perhaps they even disagree among themselves whether this postmodern paradigm is utterly new or is merely a different phase of modern consciousness.

The third type of theology is chiefly concerned with social *applicability*. Included here are the various liberationist proposals for doing theology as models of transformative praxis. *Liberationism* is a word that embraces an assortment of special-interest groups: black, feminist, Third World political theologies, and gay and lesbian activists.

All of these various types of theology realize that ultimately they must give an account of what they mean by God. Now I will describe some of the current methodological proposals that illustrate the characteristic features of each of the three types.

The most celebrated group that makes the identity principle of Christianity its chief concern is best known as the new Yale school of theology, which includes Hans Frei, George Lindbeck, David Kelsey, Ronald Thiemann, and others. Lindbeck calls this approach Anselmian scripturalism. It draws on Clifford Geertz's notion of religion as a cultural system, Ludwig Wittgenstein's rule-theory of language games, and Karl Barth's idea of doctrines as a kind of grammar book of faith. Consequently, we find here a rejection of all traditional types of natural theology, or foundationalist philosophy, or apologetic methods in order to translate the primary language of faith into some other system of language. Christian faith is like a language: you either learn to speak Christianese or you don't, and no rational natural theology about God and religion will help you do it. Finding secular allies in the neopragmatists Richard Bernstein and Richard Rorty, the Yale school of theology rejects epistemology and metaphysics as well as the long tradition of interest in method to prove the truth of religion. One of the neopragmatists, Jeffrey Stout of Princeton University, says that "preoccupation with method is like clearing your throat; it can go on for only so long before you lose your audience."[7]

The result of this alliance of theology with neopragmatism is the tendency to exchange truth for fidelity. The enterprise of fundamental theology, uncovering universal principles and structures, is surrendered in order to secure a license to operate as one voice alongside others in a pluralistic setting. It is difficult to sustain the truth-claim of the gospel and the universal mission of the church on the basis of this program for theology. Fideism is linked to relativism as theology modestly restricts itself to its own data base and leaves all other disciplines to their own devices. The weak point of this program, however, is also its

19

strength, because it keeps to the task of transmitting the texts and traditions on which all Christian faith depends for its own identity and future.

I turn now to the second type of theology, which stresses the rational intelligibility of religion and Christianity, and briefly look at the theocentric perspective of James Gustafson in theology and ethics.[8] Gustafson claims to stand in the Reformed tradition of John Calvin and Friedrich Schleiermacher, as well as Jonathan Edwards and H. Richard Niebuhr. Theology for Gustafson is grounded in the prereflective experience of religious feeling, modified by the particular piety of a historical community. The theologian's task, however, is not merely to repeat the first-order language of a tradition but to reflect critically on that tradition and its piety. In light of today's cosmology, Gustafson argues for ridding theology of its homocentric hubris and anthropomorphic images of God. Gustafson rejects as excessive the idea "that God has intelligence, like but superior to our own, and that God has a will, a capacity to control events comparable to the more radical claims made for human beings."[9] Jeffrey Stout finds Gustafson's idea of God a rather odd one for a theologian claiming to be Christian. He states: "Gustafson's desire to avoid anthropomorphic conceptions of the Deity leads him, in the end, to the view that in one important respect the Deity is more like a dog than like a human being."[10]

Gustafson's chief target is the christological focus of the doctrine of God, which he finds most pronounced in theologies based on the Reformation. Gustafson appropriates the theme of God's sovereignty from the Calvinist tradition and drives it against everything that draws God deeply into history and the human order. He pits his God of glory against the God of the gospel and, therefore, also against the doctrines of incarnation, atonement, and eternal life. All of these he dismisses as a narcissistic masquerade of self-indulging piety. He regards "the biblical claim that all things are or will be made new in Christ" as hyperbole of the heart.[11] Needless to say, Gustafson's theocentric vision of reality contains no Christology and hence no theology of the gospel at all. He has a place for Jesus, not as the incarnation of God, but as "the incarnation of theocentric piety and fidelity."[12] There is no Good Friday and no Easter Sunday. Nevertheless, Gustafson believes he has salvaged all that is appropriate from the Bible and the Christian tradition for persons who refuse to sacrifice their intellect on the altar of traditional Christianity. Gustafson and his followers claim to be the authentic heirs of John Calvin, whose infinite God of majesty supposedly enjoys neither the freedom nor the heart to enter the finite world of human flesh, suffering, and death. The God of glory (*Deus gloriosus*) in the theocentric theology of Calvin's American heirs would not assume the form of a crucified Jew from Nazareth. This is to work to the limit the Calvinist maxim that the finite cannot encompass the infinite (*finitum non capax infiniti*).

The theocentric theology of religious pluralism also bears scrutiny. Paul Knitter and John Hick are leading the way to a new pluralistic theology of world religions which places Christianity on a par with all others.[13] They applaud an evolution in Christian self-understanding in this century that has moved from ecclesiocentrism to Christocentrism to theocentrism in order to find a common denominator for all religions that tolerates no privileged position for any one. John Hick calls this a "Copernican revolution," which places God and not Christ at the center of the universe of faiths. Christ must decrease so that God might increase! As the pendulum swings away from Christ to the theocentric pole, then something other than Christ must define the meaning of God. These new theocentrists believe that Christ is a liability in the Christian dialogue with other religions. Christ divides, God unites! So Christians are urged to speak more of God, less of Christ, in order to travel more freely along the superhighways of interreligious dialogue.

The Copernican revolution reverses the direction of the movement of God's creative love toward the world. I maintain that the underlying Christology of the new theocentric pluralists is a new edition of Arianism, in which Christ stands one rung below God on the ladder of being. In Christian faith, Christocentrism underscores the identity of God who is really God. The so-called theocentric theologians have some other God in mind than the God of the gospel. By speaking of God apart from Christ so as not to scandalize people of other religions, none of these theocentric theologians appears to have any use for the doctrine of the Trinity.[14]

Another variant of theology that stresses the principle of rational intelligibility is ironically that of the deconstructionists, whose writings notoriously lack the virtues of rationality and intelligibility. The most prolific authors of deconstructionist postmodernism are Mark C. Taylor and Thomas J. J. Altizer, who seems to have as many lives as the proverbial cat. What is deconstructionism in theology?[15] Most obviously it is a theology heavily influenced by the French literary philosopher Jacques Derrida. Behind Derrida is Heidegger's reading of the history of Western thought and his proposal to get behind the meaning of being, which he called the destruction (*destruieren*) of metaphysics. If construction means putting something together to form a whole, deconstruction means taking a whole apart. Some American thinkers are fascinated with the French Heideggerians—Derrida, Foucault, Lacan, Levinas—who proclaim that the age of metaphysics is over.

The essence of deconstructionism is the rupture of the correlation between language and reality, between signs and the way things are. This leads to the suspicion that theological deconstructionists are relativists and nihilists. Mark C. Taylor writes a book that he entitles *Erring: A Postmodern A-Theology,* in which he proposes a way of thinking after the "death of God," the disappearance of the integral self, the end of history with a meaningful plot and goal, and the breakdown of the authority of the book.[16] Twenty years ago, Langdon Gilkey, in *Naming the Whirlwind,* put his finger on the problem posed by a-theistic theology: "The reality of God and so of the referent of religious language is the central point at issue." Similarly, in *Language, Logic and God,* Fredrick Ferré wrote that "without the element of *belief in* the reality of a referent designated by theological language, the distinctively religious character of this speech is sought in vain."[17]

The movement that surrenders the principle of referentiality, that is, of some correspondence between words and things, is spreading also in theological circles. There is a new kind of feminist theology that aims to join its liberationist commitment with the deconstructionist account of language and reality. Sharon D. Welch has projected a feminist theology of liberation. She begins her *Communities of Resistance and Solidarity* with a chapter entitled "The Fundamental Crisis in Christian Theology." The problem, she writes, "concerns the reality referent of Christian faith and thus of Christian theology." "Paul,

Aquinas, Luther, and Tillich assume that faith refers to something real, an experience of ultimacy that is in some way actual and present, an ultimacy that limits and shapes the nature of theological inquiry. We modern academic theologians no longer have the surety of such a referent."[18] Her critique of the more usual types of liberation theology, black and Latin American, addresses their unquestioned assumption about the reality of God and the referential truth of its language. In Welch's theology, the referent is not God but liberating praxis, not the noun but the verb, with human beings and communities the subject of the acting: "That is, the language here is true not because it corresponds with something in the divine nature but because it leads to actual liberation in history."[19]

The old ghost of Feuerbach, grinning from ear to ear, has taken charge of this theological approach, but not without assistance from a merger of American pragmatism with a neo-Marxist theory of praxis coming from liberation theology.

This feminist theology of liberation also introduces the third major type of theology, the one that presses for social relevance and applicability. The location of liberation theology is not primarily in the academy but in advocacy groups that pressure the churches to change the structures of society. The mainline churches are led by bureaucrats who either espouse the slogans of liberation theology or yield to their persistent demands. The social gospel of the old liberal theologians has been replaced by the more radical-sounding rhetoric of the liberation theologians. The challenge for the liberation theologians is not the question of atheism, whether God exists, but of idolatry, the struggle between God and competing gods, which are usually identified as capitalism and oppressive right-wing governments. The real issue for them is not the existential crisis of meaning—the luxury of the affluent classes—but the global crisis of misery, massive hunger, poverty, and oppression. Where is God? God is on the side of the poor, which, as good luck would have it, is exactly the same side on which liberation theologians happen to be. What is the gospel in this transaction? It is equated with the idealistic vision of a transformed society abounding with peace and justice—a kind of utopian dream of the kingdom brought down to earth. I believe this explains why Americans, above all, have been attracted to liberation theology. It is one more chapter in the American quest for the kingdom, only now expanded to include global dimensions. I cannot help but add that this all sounded so much more plausible before the fall of the Berlin wall and the phenomenal, peaceful revolutions in Eastern Europe in 1989 and 1990.

Sundering God and the Gospel

The picture of pluralism in American theology that we have sketched contains various images of God, but none is modeled on the God of the gospel according to the Scriptures, the Ecumenical Creeds, or the Reformation confessional writings.

Those who interpret American Christianity in light of biblical and confessional norms would perhaps go beyond Dietrich Bonhoeffer's depiction of Protestantism without a reformation. Some would speak even more harshly of apostasy in American Christianity. Perhaps those who call for a new confessing movement are so few in number that they hardly figure to be more than a little speck on the horizon of our religious and theological pluralism, but that is no reason to lose hope. A grain of mustard seed is quite small and not so imposing.

Signs appear here and there of a gathering of minds around a critique of American Christianity that rests its case on a vastly different understanding of God and the gospel. The basic issue is a christological one that results in separating God from the gospel. The fatal flaw in American Christianity can be traced back to ancient festering christological issues that were never really resolved either at Chalcedon or in the sixteenth-century controversy between Lutherans and Calvinists. In order to explain the heavy charge that American Protestantism is without a reformation yet very earnestly religious and theological in its own way, I intend to draw upon the thought of my closest American collaborator, Robert W. Jenson. As the coeditor with me of a two-volume work entitled *Christian Dogmatics,* we have attempted to promote an understanding of God that is explicated in trinitarian, christological, soteriological, ecclesiological, and sacramental doctrines that give expression to a potential reformation of Christianity on American soil.[20] As an intentionally ecumenical proposal, however, it stands in polar opposition to the plurality of models we have sketched above.

Jenson, in his recent book on Jonathan Edwards entitled *America's Theologian,* brilliantly analyzes the theological flaw in American Protestantism that allows it so easily to substitute political ideology or psychotherapeutic spirituality for the gospel. Jonathan Edwards is America's first and perhaps only truly great theologian. Currently, a renaissance of Edwardsean scholarship is under way. Most history books picture Edwards in terms of his fiery preaching about "Sinners in the Hand of an Angry God," which stirred up the Great Awakening. The rediscovery of Edwards has been stimulated by going behind the published editions of his works into material recorded only in unpublished notebooks. Jenson's account shows how American Protestantism might indeed have experienced the reformation that Bonhoeffer missed had Jonathan Edwards not lost the battles he fought against both the Arminians, whom he believed were corrupting Calvinism, and the Deists, whose rational religion was not enlightened by the beauty of the trinitarian God of the gospel. Moreover, Edwards's theological career was interrupted when at the age of fifty-five he died one month after becoming the president of Princeton.

The problem that Edwards saw with both the Arminians and the Deists was their inadequately Christian identification of God. The Christian faith disintegrated into both a deistical knowledge of God apart from the gospel and a purely sentimental subjectivistic relation to Jesus. American Protestantism has waffled back and forth between a unitarianism of the first article of the Creed and a unitarianism of the second article of the Creed without grasping how both are mutually related in the doctrine of the Trinity. When Edwards spoke of God, he always meant the specifically triune God. He did not follow the habit of his tradition that spoke first of the one God—so that the Enlightenment deists could share this common ground— and only thereafter of God as Triune, which increasingly was seen as an arbitrary piece of piety undisciplined by serious thought. Edwards's theology was radically theocentric, and thus James Gustafson can with some plausibility appeal to him. Gustafson, however, converts Edwards's theocentricity into its exact opposite, one in which there is not the beauty of the plurality of persons in God's being, in that "he subsists in three persons: Father, Son and Holy Ghost."[21] Edwards says, "God has appeared glorious to me, on account of the Trinity." When we see God in his beauty, what we see is "the glorious things of the gospel."[22]

I agree with the judgment of Robert Jenson that we met the theological crossroads of American Protestant Christianity when the constructive possibility offered by Edwards was aborted. The story of American Protestantism proceeded to run its course without a reformation, the essence of which would have been an interpretation of the nature and attributes of God based on what happened in and for the world solely through Jesus Christ as attested by the community created and sustained by the Holy Spirit. Consequently, the contributions of American Protestant theologians to the specifically Christian doctrine of the Trinity or of the person and work of Christ have been practically nil. No wonder that Sallie McFague could open her *Metaphorical Theology* with a quotation from Simone Weil's *Waiting for God:* "There is a God. There is no God. Where is the problem? I am quite sure there is no God in the sense that I am sure there is nothing which resembles what I can conceive when I say that word."[23] She goes on to comment at the end of her book, "The last word as well as the first word in theology is silence. We know with Simone Weil that when we try to speak of God there is nothing which resembles what we can conceive when we say that word."[24] In her latest book, *Models of God,* Sallie McFague follows Gordon Kaufman's idea of God as an imaginative construction of the mind, but she proposes that new metaphors for God should be drawn from the feminine sensibilities needed for a nuclear age. She substitutes a trinity of mother, lover, and friend for the traditional one of Father, Son, and Spirit. This trinitarianism describes the God–world relationship in terms of a construal of contemporary feminine experience, but it bypasses the gospel of the cross and resurrection of Jesus.[25]

The first American theologian to write a systematic construction of the Trinity is Robert Jenson.[26] He does it as an interpretation of God oriented by the gospel announcement that the crucified Jesus lives and will come again to establish God's eschatological rule and Lordship over the creation. We cannot here deal with Jenson's imaginative interpretation of the origins and development of the doctrine of the Trinity in Eastern and

Western Christianity except to say that it helps to explain the predicament of American theology. It is a christological predicament, identifiable in the precarious settlements at the Councils of Nicaea and Chalcedon, reflected throughout the medieval scholastic disputations, and resurfacing in the sixteenth-century Lord's Supper controversy. Arius's question, "How can the Logos be God, since he sleeps like a man, and weeps, and suffers?" took a similar shape in the Calvinist question "How can the Logos, being infinite, be limited by its union with the flesh?" (*totus intra carnem* and *numquam extra carnem*).

These old discussions are not dead. They come alive again in the Christology of the pluralistic theology of religions. One of these pluralists writes: "When I call this link between the finite and the infinite by the name of Christ, I am not presupposing its identification with Jesus of Nazareth. . . . Though a Christian believes that 'Jesus is the Christ' . . . this sentence is not identical to 'the Christ is Jesus.' "[27] In other words, we have saving knowledge of God through the Logos apart from Jesus, apart from the flesh of Christ (*extra carnem Christi*). Then the ground of God's revelatory and saving presence is located no longer in the enfleshed Logos but in the experience of individual believers. Then we have talk about God that is separable from the gospel. The debate whether or not God exists—between theists and atheists—goes on totally uninterpreted by the death and resurrection of Jesus. God is one subject and Jesus another, and this dichotomy leaves us in a situation from which the real incarnation of God in Jesus was meant to rescue us. The attributes of God and the attributes of Jesus the man may be exchanged *in verbo* (in words) but not *in re* (in reality), as long as such pious talk disclaims all ontological validity. What we are left with is a contemporary equivalent of Zwingli's concept of *alloeosis* (a figure of speech), about which Luther said: "It is the devil's mask."[28] Zwingli's metaphorical theology pointed to a Christ who in his human nature is separate from God. The result is a Savior who cannot save. If you can point to God where Jesus is not or to Jesus where God is not, you have a divided Christ and therefore a useless Savior. In Christ we truly do meet the humanity of God.

The old Lutherans attacked the *extra-Calvinisticum* because it placed in question faith's need to be nourished by the real presence of the total Christ whose divine and human natures cannot be separated or divided. The American heirs of the *extra-Calvinisticum* have sundered God and the gospel. The result is a "different gospel," as the apostle Paul was wont to say, "a gospel contrary to what we proclaimed to you" (Gal 1:6, 8). We will know that the Reformation has arrived in American Christianity when God and the gospel mutually interpret each other, not only to satisfy the emotional needs of Christians but also to make sense of speaking of God.

The task of theology calls for a comprehensive strategy that embraces all three concerns—identity, intelligibility, applicability. This strategy will not be possible until American theology at last develops a christocentric trinitarian monotheism that bridges the gap between its academic God-talk and its popular Jesus-piety. The laity believe in Jesus while the theologians talk about God. The problem is that there exists no theological paradigm in terms of which the academic and ecclesial publics can understand each other.

The task that needs doing calls for an ecumenical strategy. Lutherans have a special role to play, not as one denomination among others but as evangelical catholics carrying on the unfinished business of the Reformation. Its specific witness to the God of the gospel exists for the sake of renewing the whole universal church of Christ. On American soil, evangelical catholics can be found in all the denominations, but the structures to mobilize them as a movement within the churches either do not exist or are informal at best. Things may be happening, however, to raise hope for an evangelical reformation of the churches that takes seriously the special problems and possibilities of Christianity in America.

[2]

Absoluteness Is a Predicate of God's Kingdom

THE "ABSOLUTENESS OF CHRISTIANITY" is a formula that goes back to Georg W. F. Hegel's philosophy of religion, and in many places his writings refer to Christianity as the "absolute religion."[1] It is a philosophical concept that Hegel used to express what the classical Christian tradition understood by the dogma of the incarnation as well as the deep convictions of the biblical communities of both Old and New Testaments. Deut 4:39 states: "So acknowledge today and take to heart that the Lord is God in heaven above and on the earth beneath; there is no other." Acts 4:12 states: "There is salvation in no one else, for there is no other name under heaven given among mortals by which we must be saved." When Martin Luther called Christianity the true and only religion (*vera et unica religio*), he was merely passing on what virtually all Christians took for granted. The standard Protestant concept of the absoluteness of Christianity has been christocentrically expressed by the biblical verse attributed to Jesus: "I am the way, and the truth, and the life. No one comes to the Father except through me" (John 14:6). The traditional Catholic notion has been ecclesiocentrically rendered in the Cyprianic maxim that outside the church there is no salvation (*extra ecclesiam nulla salus*).

Long before Hegel, the idea of Christianity as the absolute religion was placed on shaky foundations by Gotthold Ephraim Lessing. In his famous fable of the three rings, Lessing raised the question whether Christianity is really the true religion and

29

whether there is even any way to prove it one way or another. The fable is as follows: In ancient times it was the custom for the father to give his favorite son a ring for his inheritance. The ring possessed a kind of magic power to make the one who owned it loved by God and humanity. A certain father has three sons whom he loves equally. In order to hurt none of them, he has two perfect imitations of the true ring made. Before the father dies, he gives each son his blessing along with one of the rings. Each of the three sons thinks he has the true ring and considers the others false. The three sons go to the wise judge Nathan, who becomes the spokesman for the superior counsel of Lessing himself and the new philosophy of the Enlightenment. All three rings may be false, but there's no way to tell; so Nathan offers his wise counsel: "Let each think his own is without doubt the real ring and trust that, in the long run, in a thousand thousand years, it will establish itself by the 'proof of the spirit and power.' " Meanwhile, each son should show forth "gentleness, a heart-felt tolerance, good works and deep submission to God's will."[2]

Lessing raised a number of doubts about the absoluteness of Christianity and its alleged superiority to other religions. All religions may be equally true and equally false, but the proof lies millions of years away. Anyway, the point of religion is to inculcate piety and morality, which all religions are able to do for their adherents. Christian apologetics, however, faces an "ugly big ditch" with history on one side and the absolute on the other. In Lessing's unforgettable words, "Accidental historical truths can never become proofs for necessary truths of reason."[3] In the end Lessing offered only one hope, not by any kind of historical apologetics but only through an experience of the heart. Kierkegaard's leap of faith was meant to carry him over the same nasty ditch. Kant's distinction between the phenomenal realm of space and time and the noumenal realm of God and the soul also placed history and the absolute in a sharp *diastasis* (separation). Fichte made the ditch even more hopelessly wide when he stated that it is only the metaphysical, and on no account the historical, that saves.

Hegel was unwilling to split hairs intellectually while trying to remain in touch somehow with both the historical and the absolute. He proposed a daring dialectical maneuver to unite the absolute with history in a way that would translate the basic message of New Testament Christianity into philosophical thought. He did this by putting history into the life of the absolute as something essential to its very being and self-manifestation. Hegel reformulated the doctrine of the living God in terms of trinitarian dialectics, in contrast to the abstract absolute deity of metaphysical philosophy. The true identity of the absolute mediates itself in and through the dynamic elements of history as proper to its own life.

Hegel's synthesis gave way to new forms of the old *diastasis*. The nineteenth century produced conflicting responses to the problem of the absolute religion. Orthodox supranaturalism retreated from history into an authoritarian system secured by the doctrine of the inspiration and infallibility of Scripture. The absolute in history is defined in the dogma of the incarnation, but it need not be put to the test by the historical critical method. On the other side was neo-Pietism, which postulated an immediate relation to the absolute in the depths of personal religious experience. The relativities of history neither help nor hinder the access of subjective inwardness to the essence of Christianity as a religion. A third position beyond orthodoxy and pietism was that of theological liberalism, which intended to give history its full due and to live with the implications. The result was a historicism that relativized all religions, including Christianity.

Ernst Troeltsch wrestled with the problem of historicism and its negative impact on the claim of Christianity to be the absolute religion. Troeltsch returned to Kant behind Hegel and placed theology once again in front of that ugly ditch, with an ahistorical absolute on one side and historical relativity on the other. Theology, like nature, abhors a vacuum. Troeltsch raised questions he could not answer. When he abandoned his chair in systematic theology at the University of Heidelberg in favor of a position at the University of Berlin as a philosopher of culture, he may have thereby offered a symbolic commentary on the dilemma in which he found himself as a theologian. Karl Barth spoke for many people of his era when he stated:

> Troeltsch was a gifted and, in his own way, a pious man. The same may be said of many of his great predecessors. But it was obvious that with him his *Glaubenslehre* [Troeltsch's dogmatics] was on the

point of dissolution into endless and useless talk, and that for all the high self-consciousness of its conduct Neo-Protestantism in general had been betrayed on to the rocks, or the quicksands. It was because we could no longer take part in this that about the end of the second decade of this century we left the ship. For some it was to Catholicism. . . . For others it meant a fresh beginning of serious theological study on a quite different basis.[4]

Barth realized that theology cannot go on endlessly looking back and forth between the two separate poles of the absolute and the historical; the question of the absoluteness of Christianity required a real answer. Wilfried Groll argues (in *Ernst Troeltsch und Karl Barth—Kontinuität im Widerspruch*) that Barth's radicalism presupposed Troeltsch's analysis. Barth chose to make a case for the absoluteness of Christianity, without actually using the term, by placing theology beyond the contamination of the historical virus. Consider Barth's treatment of the resurrection in his commentary on Romans:

Were there a direct and causal connexion between the historical "facts" of the resurrection—the empty tomb, for example, or the appearances detailed in I Cor. XV—and the resurrection itself; were it in any sense of the word a "fact" in history, then no profession of faith or refinement of devotion could prevent it being involved in the see-saw of "Yes" and "No" in history, life and death, God and man, which is characteristic of all that happens on the historical plane. There is under this heaven and on this earth no existence or occurrence, no transformation, be it never so striking, no experience, be it never so unique, no miracle, be it never so unheard of, which is not caught up by a relativity in which great and small are inextricably woven together. Therefore, if the resurrection be brought within the context of history, it must share in its obscurity and error and essential questionableness.[5]

Barth was thinking precisely of Troeltsch's hard lesson about the relativity of all things historical, including Christianity as a religion, the historical Jesus, and the resurrection as an event of history. Barth wanted to secure both the central place of Christianity in mediating the salvation of humankind and the absolute uniqueness of Jesus for all humanity. He realized, however, that to do so would require placing these concerns beyond the reach of history and its relativizing effects. Barth had to abandon the ship that had Troeltsch at the wheel, but he agreed with Troeltsch that history has no place for absolutes.

In a letter to Thurneysen in 1916, Barth admitted "how frightfully indifferent I have become about the purely historical questions. Of course that is nothing new for me."[6] There were others who followed Barth in jumping ship—Brunner, Bultmann, Gogarten, not to mention many Barthian disciples up to and beyond World War II. The absolute was located in the Word of God addressing us in the kerygma of proclamation. The exclusive task of theology is to think about the Word of God in its self-revelation to faith and nothing else. Dietrich Bonhoeffer rightly called this "Barth's positivism of revelation," the polar opposite of positivistic historicism. Barth simply presupposes the givenness of revelation and proceeds from that basis. What could he say, however, to the modern mind that asks for reasons to accept the Christian revelation as uniquely or absolutely revelatory in a religiously plural world, a world in which each religion claims with equal passion to possess a true and valid revelation? Along with a positivism of revelation goes the rejection of apologetics, and that implies the irrelevance of reasons, not to mention proofs. Theology is content to retreat to the sheer datum of the kerygma, the Word of God, in splendid isolation from the problems raised by the modern consciousness of history.

Barth professed to have no need to construct a rational apologetic (*wissenschaftlich*) case for the absoluteness of the Christian religion, because religion itself is defined as an affair of the godless person. Religion is unbelief, the opposite of faith. With religion rejected, no one should be concerned about either a theology of the religions or how to relate the Christian claim to the real world of religions. Bonhoeffer radicalized Barth's position. He declared that the age of religion itself had come to an end and had yielded its place—fulfilling Comte's prophecy—to the modern, secular age. Such a situation would not be serious for Christianity unless Christianity continued to misunderstand itself as a religion. True faith can thrive in a "world come of age," in which it is free at last from the chain of religious bondage. Christianity can therefore look upon the world of other religions as basically anachronistic phenomena in a technologically liberated era. Gogarten built upon this insight and attributed the rise of secularity to the radical biblical distinction between God and the world that allowed the world to be worldly, liberated from the religious powers that enthralled the ancient world. Here again Christianity is considered neither the absolute religion nor the fulfillment of the history of religions.

The Return to Troeltsch

The prospects for theology began to appear increasingly problematic as theology cut its links with philosophy, apologetics, natural theology, history, the historical method, religious experience, and world religions. A number of left-wing Barthians concluded that if the case for the absolute cannot be made under the conditions of historical human experience, then God is dead. The current wave of deconstructionism in theology (fortunately not a tidal wave but more like a ripple) admits a family resemblance with Barth's early diastatic dialectics (almost a contradiction in terms), which he expressed in the Romans commentary during his Kierkegaard-Overbeck phase. When Tillich was first asked to explain dialectical theology to his innocent American audience, he opined that dialectical theology engages in yes and no, saying yes to itself and no to everyone else. Tillich carried some battle scars for withstanding the vehement "No" of dialectical theology against his apologetic methodology, which presupposed some common ground in experience, culture, religion, philosophy, and history between Christianity and other religions or ideologies.

Strong proposals for the future of theology advocate a return to the way in which Troeltsch formulated the problem of the absoluteness of Christianity in relation to the history of religions. In 1976, the University of Lancaster, England, sponsored a colloquium on Troeltsch's intellectual legacy (out of which came a book entitled *Ernst Troeltsch and the Future of Theology*). One of the main themes dealt with the relationship of Christianity to the other religions. Long before that conference, however, Paul Tillich delivered his last public lecture, entitled "The Significance of the History of Religions for the Systematic Theologian," in which he took up Troeltsch's theme without even mentioning his name—perhaps a sign that the power of neoorthodoxy had caused people to forget about Troeltsch. The situation after World War II, when traffic increased from the Eastern religions into a traditionally Christian

West, generated a new awareness of Christianity's encounter with other world religions. The claim that the Christian message is something totally other in comparison to other religions, that Christian theology may legitimately operate in isolation from the general historical scientific study of the religions, proved to be less and less sustainable.

Ernst Benz was one of the first to challenge the neoorthodox strategy of quarantining Christianity from exposure to the history of religions. In his programmatic essay "Ideas for a Theology of the History of Religion," Benz stated: "One of the urgent tasks of contemporary theology is to formulate a new theological understanding of the history of religion."[7] The idea of an absolute discontinuity between Christianity and other religions, which found its expression in dialectical theology, must be challenged today. In the same vein, Wolfhart Pannenberg argues, in his essay "Toward a Theology of the History of Religions,"[8] that the other religions of the world are a permanent presupposition of the universal missionary mandate inherent in Christianity from the beginning. He maintains that Christianity's promise of future fulfillment through the gospel of Christ would be meaningless apart from the universal context of the religious history of humanity.

On the ecumenical front, the World Council of Churches published "Guidelines on Dialogue with People of Living Faiths and Ideologies," and after the Second Vatican Council, the Roman Catholic Church established a special department to seek cooperation with the non-Christian religions. Dialogues are springing up all over the world!

In North America, theology is being challenged by a welter of viewpoints that bring Christianity into a history-of-religions framework. I refer to the seminal works of scholars like Wilfrid Cantwell Smith, John Hick, John Cobb, and Paul Knitter.[9]

The combined impact of these movements and thinkers has impelled theologians to take a new look at the thought of Ernst Troeltsch. Pannenberg writes:

> Among the Christian theologians of this century who were concerned with preventing the Christian religion and Christian theology from wandering down sectarian byways, out of touch with the general development of culture, Ernst Troeltsch is today the outstanding figure. . . . His formulations of the problems and tasks

with which he confronted Christian thought have not lost their validity and their capacity for clarifying issues.[10]

If the strategy of assuming the absoluteness of Christianity in sectarian isolation from the rest of the world—from philosophy, history, and science—is no longer acceptable, at least to many concerned about the future of theology, then it seems advisable to reopen the discussion at the point where it was cut off. If we take Troeltsch's formulation of the problem as a point of departure, then we might see more clearly some of the paths that lead forward from that starting point.

Troeltsch became convinced that he was participating in a revolution taking place in Christianity and, therefore, in Christian theology as well. In 1900 he wrote a letter to his friend Adolf von Harnack, in which he states: "It is not merely a new theology that we espouse and teach, but indeed a completely new phase of Christianity itself."[11] In *The Absoluteness of Christianity and the History of Religions,* Troeltsch described the factor of change and novelty as "the development of an unreservedly historical view of human affairs."[12] The modern idea of history puts an end to the naive certainty that Christianity holds a normative position among the religions. It also, according to Troeltsch, does away with Hegel's comprehensive theory of Christianity as the absolute religion in relation to the relative truths of all non-Christian religions. Hegel's evolutionary apologetic is closely related to the orthodox apologetic in that they both place Christianity in a uniquely normative position. Troeltsch's verdict: "It is impossible to construct a theory of Christianity as the absolute religion on the basis of a historical way of thinking or by the use of historical means."[13] Christianity is a completely historical phenomenon radically conditioned by the historical situation in which it emerged as well as by the historical factors involved in its further development. Someone has called Troeltsch the Heraclitus of modern theology. Everything in the Christian religion is interwoven with the fabric of its ongoing historical environment, and historical reality itself shatters every attempt to interpret Christianity as the absolute religion.

Schleiermacher's approach was deemed no more successful than Hegel's. The absoluteness of Christianity for Schleiermacher was reduced to a single point, the person of Jesus, whom he pictured as absolute, unconditioned, in his very being beyond change and suffering. Everything else proceeding from this person, however, is subject to the laws of history and its development. To this, D. F. Strauss replied that history has no place for either absolute religions or absolute personalities. Troeltsch agreed, and he believed that historical research had proved him right: "Increasingly refined historical inquiry has led to a more vital apprehension of the historically conditioned uniqueness of Christianity and to a more and more radical interweaving of the Christian religion into human history generally."[14]

The Ritschlian approach was equally dubious. Ritschl used the historical method to focus on Christianity in its particular individuality in order to discover thereby that the uniqueness of Christianity lies precisely in making its claim to absolute truth and validity over every other religion. Christian theology then takes the result of historical research and adopts it as the presupposition of its work, thus subverting the historical method itself. This ecclesial approach to scholarship (*kirchliche Wissenschaft*) became the loophole that dialectical theology needed.

If Christianity is a purely historically relative phenomenon, what is then to prevent us from slipping into an absolute relativism? Troeltsch said that even though there are no absolutes in history, still there are norms pulsating through the religions that become part of one's personal value system as a matter of free choice, which makes it possible to draw some relative distinctions between the religions. Troeltsch assured his frightened readers that they could still combine a radically historical way of thinking with the idea that Christianity is the highest religious truth relevant to their European cultural situation. The value of this consolation is that Christianity may be acknowledged as the highest religion as long as we admit that it is only a matter of personal conviction and not of anything inherently absolute. This admission of the completely historical character of Christianity can allow "a calm and joyful affirmation of Christianity."[15] What Troeltsch allowed under the conditions of historical relativism is that one may continue to appreciate Christianity as the highest religion as long as one adopts it as a criterion to evaluate other religions. That is equally true, however, of every other religion's self-understanding and approach. All we can say then is that Christianity is the highest religion so far, but no proof exists that it will be the final religion for all time to come.

The Copernican Revolution

Today, John Hick is carrying Troeltsch's relativistic interpretation of Christianity to an extreme, with uncompromising consistency. In a number of his writings, Hick has announced a "Copernican revolution" in theology, and he usually gives the impression that he is the pioneering spirit of this revolution. This revolution consists in a shift "from the dogma that Christianity is at the centre to the realization that it is *God* who is at the centre, and that all the religions of mankind, including our own, serve and revolve around him.[16] Hick is advocating a shift from an ecclesiocentric and christocentric view to a theocentric view of the religions.

There is usually a time lag of one or two generations between British and Continental theology. Hick's venture into demythologizing began with *The Myth of God Incarnate,* which was published in 1977, about 35 years after Bultmann's essay *New Testament and Mythology;* and he gives no noticeable trace of having advanced the terms of the discussion. Hick's "Copernican revolution" comes about seventy years after Troeltsch declared that it is hard to imagine from a modern historical perspective that the christological center of our own religious history constitutes the sole center of the history of religions: "That looks far too much like the absolutising of our own contingent area of life. That is in religion what geocentricism and anthropocentricism are in cosmology and metaphysics. The whole logic of christocentricism places it with these other centricisms."[17]

Hick uses "paradigm shift" as another term for "Copernican revolution." This term refers to a shift from a Christianity-centered or Christ-centered model to a God-centered model giving all religions equal footing. Troeltsch precisely made this point in his prophecy that Christianity was now entering upon a radically new phase. The principles of historical relativism have since become so widely assimilated by people working toward a comprehensive theology of the religions that Hick seems unaware that his relativism is a popularized reissue of Troeltsch's "Copernican revolution." It is a sheer return to a pre-Barthian theology of the history-of-religions school, and it does not acknowledge any gains or benefits from the Barthian critique of religion or the broader neo-Reformation hermeneutical retrieval of the gospel character of the New Testament message.

Hick's version of the "Copernican revolution" lacks the fullness and complexity of Troeltsch's vision. Consider this pious confession: "That Jesus is my Lord and Savior is language like that of a lover, for whom his Helen is the sweetest girl in the world."[18] The ontological grounding of the traditional claim to absoluteness, whether in reference to Christ or to his church, has now become nothing more than a linguistic product of a peculiar view stemming from private experience. Above all, Christians should no longer claim absoluteness for any of the central events that constitute their faith.

The theme of historical relativism asserts that history has no place for absolutes. Paul Knitter stands in the forefront of Catholics who promote the Copernican revolution as it concerns Christianity and the religions. Knitter sees that Buddhism today is compelling Christians to "ask whether their traditional claims that Jesus is exclusively unique or even inclusively unique are accurate."[19] In the same vein, Knitter calls for a distinction between the mythic Christ and the historical Jesus; "for it is primarily the Mythic Christ, not the historical Jesus, who is Savior."[20] He sees that this is the tie that binds a number of contemporary christologies together, including those of Tillich, Macquarrie, Cobb, Pittenger, Ogden, Tracy, and Panikkar. All of these theologians appeal to a Logos principle that can be known and salvifically experienced as the Christ outside the flesh (*asarkos*), with Jesus becoming one among many mediators of illumination. Whether Knitter is being fair to all these thinkers in pushing them into a kind of Docetism or Gnosticism is another question, but he does show that the surest way to rid Christianity of its claim to uniqueness is to loosen the links between the Jesus-event and the Christ-principle.

Karl Jaspers had previously offered the same counsel in his *Philosophical Faith and Revelation*. If there is a central event in world history, it is not the one that divides B.C. from A.D. but, rather, concentrates the events that constitute the "axial age," the age in which the human spirit on different continents broke through to a new spiritual and more personal awareness of the Eternal One. This axial period runs from about 800 to 200 B.C.

and includes Confucius in China, Gautama (Buddha) in India, Zoroaster in Persia, and the great Hebrew prophets in Israel. Christianity is a later offshoot of Judaism and not a fundamentally new and different religious option. From this broad, sweeping historical perspective, we can see how incongruous it seems for any one of the religions to claim to be absolute.

In Jaspers, we find a contemporary statement of the Copernican revolution that Troeltsch envisioned and that is now being reenvisioned by Hick, Knitter, Smith, and a growing number of others. At its heart is a relativistic formulation of the meaning of religion that is hospitable to Christianity too, but only on the condition that it abandon every claim to absoluteness, particularly one that incorporates history into its life and essence. Jaspers writes:

> Whenever faith has claimed exclusive truth, the results have been discord and life-or-death struggles. . . . Not till the poison of exclusive claims is removed can the biblical faith come to be communicative, peaceful, and truly in earnest about its pure realization. . . . Removing the poison consciously takes a simple yet momentous insight: that exact, generally valid truth is relative, dependent on premises and methods of cognition but compelling for every intellect, while existential truth is historic, absolute in each man's life but not to be stated as valid for all others. Exclusiveness must fall so that the appearance of faith may come to be true to its essence—so that the struggle of ciphers may be pure, tolerant, candid, and free from the constant admixture of worldly concerns.[21]

The philosophy of history that runs from Troeltsch to Jaspers makes use of the historical method to dehistoricize the Christian faith, to dichotomize history and revelation, and to remove the absolute from involvement in the affairs of history. Perhaps the right word for this tendency in this Copernican revolution is neo-Gnosticism, because it indicates both that the religious element in this movement is as old as ancient Christianity's most serious rival and that it has little or nothing to do with Copernicus, or the modern scientific worldview, or the factual results of the historical-critical method.

History and the Eschatological Absolute

In an essay, "Troeltsch and Christian Theology," Robert Morgan has referred to Wolfhart Pannenberg as the "finest contemporary spokesman"[22] of Troeltsch's kind of historical theology. Pannenberg's thinking, however, does not fit the relativistic model espoused by Hick's Copernican revolution. The return to Troeltsch in contemporary theology has been moved mostly by the strong case he made for the incorporation of Christianity into the history of religions and by the principles of historical relativism that he articulated. Pannenberg has seen another side of Troeltsch, overlooked by most others. Pannenberg's interpretation of Troeltsch provides contemporary theology with a starting point for a different way to respond to Tillich's call to integrate systematic theology and the history of religions.

Troeltsch wrote *The Absoluteness of Christianity and the History of Religions* at a time when Johannes Weiss and Albert Schweitzer were making theology aware of the eschatological character of Jesus' proclamation of the kingdom of God. Troeltsch wrote: "In Jesus' preaching the Kingdom is the absolute."[23] The problem of the relation between history and the absolute can be reformulated by a theology conscious of eschatology as the problem of the relation between the kingdom of God and history. Pannenberg judges that this is what Troeltsch began to do:

> J. Weiss's realization of the influence of a futuristic eschatology on the message of Jesus and in particular on his idea of the kingdom of God had been revolutionary, and Troeltsch was perhaps the only systematic theologian who could incorporate it into his theology without losing sight of the real futurity of the rule of God. Opposing supernaturalist assertions of an absolute within history, he was able to base his argument on the fact that Jesus himself had consigned "absolute religion" to "the world to come."[24]

Another quotation from Pannenberg: "Troeltsch appealed to the power 'of the eschatological idea the influence of which is now universally admitted to extend throughout the Gospel' and which he called 'the magnificent expression of the unique value of the religious purpose.' "[25]

In other words, we find Troeltsch saying that if we take as our clue Jesus' own view of the kingdom, the absolute belongs essentially to the future end of history. Even Jesus distinguished between the absolute future of the kingdom and his own person. In this sense, therefore, history as such contains no absolute; the truth of historical relativism is not abrogated by the idea of the kingdom as the absolute future.

41

The point at which Pannenberg becomes critical has to do with the way in which Troeltsch connected the future to the present. For Troeltsch, the connection is teleological, established by the category of purpose. For Pannenberg, however, the

> category of purpose which is so central for Troeltsch does not fit the eschatology of the kingdom of God, because in Jesus' message the coming kingdom is not an extension of human purposes, but comes without any human intervention. . . . Moreover, the influence of the category of final purpose makes Troeltsch give a one-sided emphasis to the kingdom of God as something in the future, at the expense of the presence of this future in the history of Jesus, an aspect to which he allows only passing significance. Connected with this must also be Troeltsch's inability completely to escape from the difficulties of relativism. Precisely because his idea of the absolute was a final goal in the sense of something totally beyond the present experience of history, present experience in his account necessarily lacks the absolute: its truth lies outside itself.[26]

Despite this limitation, Pannenberg can urge a reconsideration of Troeltsch's understanding of history, because Troeltsch was able to give a place to the future-oriented eschatology of primitive Christianity: "This thesis of Troeltsch's, which even today has lost none of its central validity, may be regarded as one of his most significant contributions to theology. If from the outset it had received the acceptance it deserves, the theology of this century could have avoided many detours."[27] Clearly, dialectical theology, particularly its thesis of discontinuity between Christianity and other religions, is one of the detours.

Why did dialectical theology find no future for theology in Troeltsch's thought? The answer is chiefly for the reason that Pannenberg mentions: Troeltsch's inability to relate the absolute future of the kingdom in a positive way to Jesus' own person and achievement. For Troeltsch, Jesus placed the absolute in the future kingdom, whereas primitive Christianity transferred this absoluteness to the person of Jesus and endowed him with such titles as Messiah, Lord, and Savior. Troeltsch's Christology failed to produce a criterion of what is distinctively Christian. Barth and company jumped ship, and whatever merit attached to Troeltsch's idea of the future kingdom as the eschatological absolute was left behind.

I would prefer not to look upon the period of dialectical theology as an unnecessary detour. Theology must at times withdraw from syntheses and correlations with philosophical systems and religious worldviews, withdraw in order to enter upon a holding operation for the sake of concentrating on the sacred texts and retrieving classic memories from forgotten or forsaken traditions. A detour was bound to happen in the movement from dialectical theology into the later phases of biblical theology and neoorthodoxy because the Troeltschian style of religious-scientific study led to what Barth called "endless and useless talk." Troeltsch himself pondered whether his interpretation of absoluteness "can satisfy ordinary religious people whose modes of perception are those of the modern world, and above all whether it can serve our clergymen and theologians. . . . The question to be considered now is whether this kind of absoluteness can provide them with a foundation from which they can derive encouragement as they carry on their work."[28] Barth, of course, said "No," and history seemed to prove him correct in the trials that were to come.

The question we face today is whether the crisis of theology calls for a new theology of crisis. Currently, Eberhard Jüngel is continuing the Barthian approach of the "Word alone." In *God as the Mystery of the World,* Jüngel comments:

> There are two approaches in contemporary theology by which the attempt is being made to learn to think God again. The one way, pursued by Wolfhart Pannenberg with impressive consequentiality, is to think "God having been removed" (*remoto deo*) in order to arrive at the disclosure of the thought of God which then functions as the framework for the Christian faith's own understanding of God. The studies in this book will take the opposite approach. The thinking here pursues a path which, one might say, goes from the inside toward the outside, from the specifically Christian faith experience to a concept of God which claims universal validity. The goal of the intellectual route adopted in this book is not to demonstrate the thinkability of God on the basis of general anthropological definitions, but rather to think God and also man on the basis of the event of God's self-disclosure which leads to the experience of God, and thus to demonstrate that the Christian truth is universally valid on the basis of its inner power.[29]

Jüngel sees clearly that the line forward from Troeltsch through Tillich to Pannenberg is based on premises diametrically opposed to his own. We can summarize them as follows: (1)

Religion is universally human; it is a structural dimension of human existence. (2) Revelation is experienced in the positive religions of humanity. (3) Christianity is a religion that lays claim to the absolute significance of God's revelation in Jesus Christ. (4) The task of theology is to interpret the history of religions in light of Christology. The movement of thought is generally from below to above, and it goes from the outside to the inside. This is the question-answer model common to all apologetic theology. It presupposes that reason, no matter how wounded by sin, is able to think its way toward God, in search of its own absolute ground and goal. Tillich, in *Biblical Religion and the Search for Ultimate Reality,* put it this way: "Against Pascal I say: The God of Abraham, Isaac, and Jacob and the God of the philosophers is the same God."[30] There is an "elenctical use of reason" which leads reason to its limit and asks for what lies beyond its reach, parallel to the "elenctical use of the law" which drives the sinner toward the gospel.[31]

Jüngel has not followed this line of reasoning. Like Barth, he rejects the way of natural theology or, as it is more commonly called today, fundamental theology. He rejects any rational grounding which precedes faith. He asserts: "For too much, not too little [!], speaks for the reasonableness of God's revelation and of faith in him for it to be rational to provide a rational foundation for that reasonableness."[32] Is Jüngel taking us back to Lessing's "ugly ditch" between Christianity and the Enlightenment, theology and philosophy, faith and religion, revelation and history? He writes: "For Christian theology can use the word 'God' meaningfully only in a context which is defined by the understanding of the human person of Jesus. Whatever the word 'God' is to mean for our thinking is determined, for the Christian faith, in Jesus. Faith understands and confesses him as the word of God."[33] "The presupposition is that ultimately only the speaking God himself can say what the word 'God' should provide us to think about. Theology comprehends this whole subject with the category of revelation."[34]

These quotations really mean that there is no point to an integration of Christian theology and the history of religions. Whatever other religions may mean by "God" is their own affair. There is no point of contact in religion, history, or experience. Jüngel is in dialogue with Western secular atheism. There is no sign that he is thinking on the basis of an encounter with believing people in other great religious traditions. The contrast between Jüngel and Pannenberg places theology before a sharply defined "either/or." Pannenberg starts with anthropology and seeks from there to demonstrate the necessity of God. What other religions, therefore, mean by "God" is grounded in a common universal anthropological orientation to the absolute ground and goal of human existence. Jüngel juxtaposes to this anthropological starting point the thesis of the "worldly nonnecessity of God."[35] This has a Bonhoefferian ring: "Man can be human without God. He can speak, hear, think, and act without speaking about God, without perceiving God, without thinking of God, without working for him. And he can do all of that very well and with great responsibility. The human person can well live without God, can listen attentively, think acutely, act responsibly."[36]

Jüngel establishes the absoluteness of Christianity by a process of excluding from everything that which does not constitute the event on which Christianity is based: that is, God revealed in the contradiction of the cross of Jesus Christ. Here we have the heart of Luther's concern: *crux sola est nostra theologia*. As Martin Kähler said, "The cross is the basis and test of all real theology."[37] For Jüngel, this means that "God is not necessary in a worldly sense, that God is groundless in a worldly sense."[38]

Where is Jüngel coming from? He is coming from Luther, Hegel, and Barth. Here is the puzzle (which deserves to be explored by a doctoral dissertation or two): Jüngel appeals to Hegel and so does Pannenberg, each with equal passion and conviction. Jüngel writes:

> Not only in the metaphysical tradition but in the Christian as well, the concept of the divine being has been so dominated by the thought of absoluteness that to think of the christological identity of God with the crucified Jesus at best could lead only to a paradox which bursts all thought apart. That God's being does not contradict itself in the crucified man Jesus, but rather harmonizes with itself, was at most stated but certainly not thought through. It was the older Barth who, in this regard, dared to pursue resolutely the path which had been opened up by Luther and Hegel—the theological public has largely failed to notice this.[39]

For Jüngel, Christ—the crucified Christ—provides the occasion for speaking of God as triune. For Pannenberg also,

Christology is the basis for speaking of the three persons in the unity of God.[40] What then is the difference? Jenson has given us the benefit of his opinion in *The Triune Identity:* Karl Barth has developed a christological inversion of Hegel's idea of the Trinity. In Hegel, Jenson says, the world is God's Object rather than Jesus. With Barth you have only to put Jesus in place of Hegel's "world," and you have Barth's doctrine of the Trinity[41]; and that is exactly what Jüngel does. Barth will have nothing to do with the ancient patristic idea that there are vestiges of the Trinity (*vestigia trinitatis*) throughout the history of religions. In his newly published systematic theology, Pannenberg relates the christologically grounded doctrine of the Trinity to the knowledge of God in the other world religions. Their experience and understanding of the reality of God are not void of theological significance. He does not, however, collapse the unique revelation of God in Christ into the general experience of divine revelation in the non-Christian religions.

Jesus Christ as Religions' Fulfillment

Many and various are the schemes to link Christianity and the non-Christian religions. They include, among others, Rahner's "anonymous Christianity," Tillich's "latent church," Schlette's distinction between the ordinary ways of salvation within the world religions and the extraordinary way within the Catholic church, and the scholastic theory of a "second chance" in the next life. All such artificial "loopholes" can be avoided if one goes along with Hick's Copernican revolution and declares that all religions have their own saving mediators and that Jesus Christ is but one of them. If, however, the particularity of salvation in Christ is somehow causally efficacious for the world, it is inevitable that Christian theology will speculate on the means by which such efficacy becomes experientially concrete and universal. A theology that arbitrarily discounts the claim to absoluteness implied by the exclusive monotheism of the Bible as well as the claim to universal validity inherent in the apostolic gospel can hardly serve credibly as a representative of Christian faith in dialogue with other religions.

Commitment to the God of the Bible and God's eschatological self-revelation in the person of Jesus Christ offers a perspective on the meaning of the absolute claim of Christianity.

I do not mean merely that God is absolute while all religions, including Christianity, are relative, being limited human answers to the divine revelation. Nor do I mean merely that Jesus Christ is absolute and that the church is relative, being nothing more than a human institution. Nor do I mean merely that the kerygmatic Word is absolute and that faith as a human response is relative. Absoluteness is rather a predicate of the God of the eschatological kingdom proclaimed by Jesus as the power of the universal future in relation to the whole of God's creation, which includes the entire sweep of the history of religions. The presence of the eschatological kingdom in Jesus and in the apostolic mission is the anticipation of the future of all religions as well as the entire religious life of humanity. These other religions are not striving after nothingness or false gods. They are looking toward union with the divine mystery that the Christian gospel announces is ultimately the same divine reality as that revealed in the person of Jesus.

The task of the Christian mission is to interact with other religions so as to bring about an encounter of all the religious traditions of humankind with the Christian message. Such an encounter presupposes that all religions, including Christianity as a religion, are open to transformation toward a future that may accomplish the kind of fulfilling and universal unity stored up in the promises of the kingdom of God. A Christian tradition wholly fixed on itself, closed to its own further transformation, and satisfied to be the religion of any particular era or region would forfeit its right to be a servant and sign of the still outstanding eschatological future of all the religions. The history of religions is still under way. Their final meaning can be discovered neither in their past nor in their limited present, but only in the end toward which they are historically moving through forces beyond their control. One aim of the Christian mission is to create space in the other religions for a future that will not negate but will fulfill them in accordance with the revelation of the divine love and mercy revealed in the ministry of Jesus and the apostolic mission.

This missionary reading of the meaning of absoluteness contradicts an interpretation that would see Christianity as something perfect and complete in itself. The claim to absoluteness is more like a mission-project to be worked out in the tension-field of history than it is a dogmatic postulate floating in the abstract. The Christian claim is not a proposition that can be proved true or false by arguments taken from Scripture or tradition; it is proving itself rather in the concrete historical process, under the conditions of world historical encounters with other religions and worldviews. Christian mission does not point to the nameless and faceless absolute of metaphysical philosophy, that static identity existing motionless and emotionless above time and history.

Absoluteness seen in terms of the universal mission to the nations does not pit Christianity against other religions as enemies of the gospel. Rather, they can be seen as realities in quest of the absolute future announced by the gospel. The Christian attitude is neither one of intolerance nor one of laisser-faire indifference. It is one of engaged interest in how God providentially has been preparing other religions to encounter the finality of the eschatological kingdom announced by Jesus and the gospel and sacramentally embodied within the community of believers.

[3]

Christ Alone
Is the Heart of
the Church's Message

THERE APPEARS TO BE A RENAISSANCE of interest in the theology of Karl Barth. For a long time in the United States we have suffered from a woeful ignorance of his real teaching. In an age of fads and paperback theology, not many take the time to embrace the whole of *Church Dogmatics* from the earliest to the latest developments—a tragedy, because Barth's theology has often been condemned to lead a pathetic existence only in the form of caricatures. Otherwise serious theologians feel justified in disposing of Barth's challenge to theology through unseemly caricatures.

Especially fashionable is caricaturing Barth's christocentric theology of salvation and its implications for the religions of the world. In dealing with Barth's theology of Christianity and the world religions, John Hick says: "Such sublime bigotry could only be possible for one who had no real interest in or awareness of the wider religious life of mankind. For it is evident, when one witnesses worship within the great world faiths, including Christianity, that the same sort of thing is going on in each."[1] In a doctoral thesis by a Roman Catholic, Colm O'Grady, the stereotypical question is posed: "But why does Barth refuse to allow that the reconciling and revealing Lord of the Church is already operative in the world, and in non-Christian religions?"[2] In his *What Are They Saying about Christ and World Religions?* Lucien Richards transmits the usual caricature under the title "Karl Barth and Christomonism." According to this caricature, "to give extra-Christian religion a theological meaning is to betray the unique role of Christ."[3] It is interesting that Protestant liberals and progressive Roman Catholics make the common accusation that Barth takes a completely condemnatory attitude toward all non-Christian religions and locates salvation too narrowly in Jesus Christ, the one Word of God. Protestant liberals and progressive Catholics teach that people can find salvation adequately in all the religions and that, for the vast majority, salvation apart from faith in Christ is the ordinary way of salvation.

At the other end of the spectrum are the evangelicals worried about Barth's universalism, in which the gateway of salvation is so wide open that, in due time, all the prodigals of the world will come home to the awaiting Father. Something seems to be enviably right about a position that counts liberals and conservatives among its harshest critics. Maybe, as Barth always suspected, Protestant liberals and traditional Catholics are sibling rivals under the skin. Barth detected a common heresy underlying them that takes a variety of forms: *analogia entis* (analogy of being), works-righteousness, natural theology, and mystical or moralistic ladders to heaven.

Barth as a Christocentric Trinitarian

The first article of the Barmen Declaration captured the christocentric accent of Barth's theology. During a tense time for the church, which was in the throes of a great struggle, Karl Barth opposed the rise of German Christianity during the Third Reich and declared with the confessing church that "Jesus Christ, as he is testified to us in the Holy Scripture, is the one Word of God, whom we are to hear, whom we are to trust and obey in life and death." The confession goes on to say: "We repudiate the false teaching that the church can and must recognize yet other happenings and powers, images and truths as divine revelation alongside this one Word of God, as a source of her preaching."[4]

In a totally different context, Christians on the American scene are facing a new church struggle. This struggle is not nearly as dramatic as the totalitarian threat of the blatant pagan ideology encountered in Hitler's National Socialism, yet it is one which strikes with equal force against the identity of Jesus Christ and the integrity of his church. We are now reaching an advanced stage of neopaganism in Europe and North America. Neopaganism can present itself in crass political, economic, and military terms; but it can also assume the guise of popular religion and new-age spirituality. "Other happenings and powers, images and truths" on the American scene compete with the one Word of divine revelation in Jesus Christ, whom we are to hear, trust, and obey in life and death. These other powers and truths are flourishing in all the mainline denominations today.

I see, however, the advent of a new church struggle that calls for the kind of clarity and courage exhibited by the confessing Christians at Barmen in 1934, a struggle against the trend in both Protestant and Catholic theology to make Christ both small and unimportant. Many books and articles on the subject of Christology have been published in the last decade or two, and a large number of them represent an anti-Barthian backlash. For Karl Barth, Jesus Christ was at the center of Christian faith and theology because he was the one Word of God whom we are to fear, trust, and obey. The Barthian christocentric emphasis is now rapidly becoming a minority opinion among the leaders of modern-Protestant and Catholic-progressive theology, just as it was during the church's struggle (*Kirchenkampf*) in the 1930s. According to these pacesetters of theology, Barth's theology is too exclusivistic; and by accentuating historical relativity and religious pluralism, many are challenging the place of Christ as the salvific center of all religions. Is Christ really that final, definitive, and normative?

John Hick represents the liberal Protestant view that allows Christians to hold to Christ as their unique Savior without necessarily claiming as much for others. Christ may be my personal Lord and Savior, but this does not mean that he is the only savior or the only lord for all other religions. To cling to Christ as the one and only Word of God, as Barth and the Barmen Declaration assert, is branded "theological fundamentalism," which modern Christianity is now, at last, outgrowing. There is room, after all, for other savior figures in other religions, at least enough to go around for everybody. To be sure, Jesus is one of the ways in which God meets the world of human experience; but it is arrogant bigotry to claim, as Barth does, that

Jesus is God's unique way of dealing with the salvation of the world.

Other voices in modern theology, like Tom Driver, Rosemary Reuther, and Dorothy Sölle, are claiming that the uniqueness, normativity, and finality of Jesus Christ account for the sins of Christianity—its sexism, racism, and anti-Semitism. The scandal of particularity that insists on a once-for-all Christ is supposedly the breeding ground of intolerance, supremacy, imperialism, and what these theologians call "Christo-fascism." As Tom Driver says, "The infinite commitment of God to finitude in Jesus does not indicate something done once and once for all time."[5] These theologians are asking for a paradigm shift from a theology in which Christ is the center to one in which he is one of the satellites in a galaxy of religious superstars. In promoting his Copernican revolution, John Hick uses Karl Barth's Christology as the best example of the old Ptolemaic system of geocentric thinking, which imagines that the incarnate revelation of God in Christ stands at the center of the universe of the world religions. Paul Knitter, speaking in favor of this new trend, states: "We are in the midst of an evolution from Christocentrism to theocentrism."[6] James Gustafson continues the attack on Christocentrism by demanding that the homocentric view that focuses on God's humanity in the earthly Christ must give way to a theocentric perspective that fits a post-Copernican view of the universe.[7]

I agree with Paul Knitter's assessment that there is a "growing endorsement" of a "nonnormative Christology" among both Protestant and Catholic theologians; however, there is a counter-offensive going on in contemporary theology sparked by interest in Karl Barth's christocentric trinitarianism. Diametrically opposed to the antichristological trend is a movement to continue the Barthian initiative toward a new affirmation of the Trinity on the basis of Christology. New books on the Trinity by Eberhard Jüngel, Jürgen Moltmann, Wolfhart Pannenberg, and Robert W. Jenson represent a significant advance toward a new conception of the Trinity. Their writings appear precisely at a time when many other theologians have raised the white flag of surrender and now look upon the Trinity as a piece of moribund speculation, which follows Harnack's verdict in his *History of Dogma* that the Trinity is a product of the acute Hellenization of Christianity. These new post-Barthian theologies of the Trinity, however, argue that the Trinity is far from being a mere memory aid to organize various topics of Christian belief (Schleiermacher's approach) and that the root of the doctrine lies deep in biblical soil, in the divinely revealed economy of salvation. The Trinity is an indispensable and integral part of the Christian comprehension of God, and it is neither an arbitrary set of metaphors that can be exchanged for more suitable ones nor a system of archaic symbols which can be translated into contemporary ideas with a bit of hermeneutical legerdemain.[8]

Why the Trinity, after all? The reason is that the identity of God is not separable from the integrity of his actions. We do not look for the inner nature of God in some remote sphere above and beyond the structure of his operations in and upon the world. A theology which begins its doctrine of God with trinitarian dialectics, as Karl Barth proposed, is the only way of speaking faithfully of the God of the gospel of Good Friday and Easter Sunday. The triune identity of God, as Jenson states, is revealed in the person of the crucified and risen Jesus; and there is no other Word of God whom we are to hear, trust, and obey in life and in death. The identification of God with the crucified Jesus drives theology to be serious about the trinitarian distinctions in God as Father, Son, and Holy Spirit. Then it no longer makes sense to speak of God in a simple untrinitarian way, as the attackers of Christocentrism try to do. As Luther said when he repudiated Zwingli's metaphorical theology and dubbed his concept of *alloeosis* the devil's mask: "It will finally construct a kind of Christ after whom I would not want to be called a Christian."[9]

Barth on Religion and the Religions

I have opened this presentation on Barth's concept of Christ and the world religions with a discussion of his doctrine of the Trinity because it holds the key to everything Barth says about God and the world, revelation and religion, and Christianity and world religions.

A distinction between Barth's earlier and later periods in speaking of the world religions can be observed. I am not prepared to argue that he changed his mind or contradicted himself, nor can I claim that he repeated himself. His thought on the relation between Christ and the world underwent some kind of development. The caricatures of Barth's theology are mostly based on the earlier period when Barth juxtaposed the absolute transcendence of God with all things creatural and worldly below. The divine and the human are contrasted: "God is in heaven and man is on earth." Barth, however, gradually came to realize what he expressed with ever-increasing confidence, that the absolute transcendence of God holds within itself the power and freedom to include itself and the whole creation. Barth moved away from the idea of exclusive transcendence in his *The Epistle to the Romans* to the idea of inclusive transcendence in his *Church Dogmatics*. Here Barth spoke of the religions in the light of Jesus Christ. Because he spoke of the religions exclusively in the light of Jesus Christ, his critics have concluded that Barth took a wholly negative approach to the non-Christian religions. Is this a justifiable and inevitable conclusion from what Barth said? Barth's view (stated clearly in par. 17 of vol. 1, part 2 of *Church Dogmatics*) is that the reality of revelation is solely a predicate of God's activity, and it cannot be reached from the side of human religions. The reality of revelation is not a cooperative affair, so much stemming from the world of God and so much from the world of religion. The human being has no capacity to reach revelation from the side of religion.

Paul Althaus and others have accused Barth of Christomonism. Is this a fair charge? Has not Barth continued the Reformation attack on synergism, works-righteousness in the sphere of religion, only to draw out more explicitly the implications of monergism from the locus of justification for an understanding of Christ in relation to all the religions of the world? A person can be saved neither by the Christian religion nor by any other world religion. People in all religions are in the same situation. They are in need of God's revelation in Jesus Christ. In Jesus Christ, God has offered the gift of himself; he has offered his grace; he has done this in the reality of Jesus Christ and nowhere else. No such revelation, no such salvation, exists anywhere else. The unbridgeable rift between the divine and the human can be overcome only through God's unique revelation in Christ. God speaks his word of revelation in the world through Christ and through no other medium. Whatever negative words Barth has to say about religion and the religions in this early period are a positive function of his axiom that outside of Christ there is no revelation of God.

Many readers of Barth have been scandalized by his harsh statements about religion, such as: "Religion is unbelief, idolatry, self-righteousness. . . . It is an affair of the godless man."[10] They often fail, however, to mention the other side of the dialectic, where Barth says: "Religion and the religions must be treated with a tolerance which is informed by the forbearance of Christ, which derives therefore from the knowledge that by grace God has reconciled to Himself godless man and his religion. It will see man carried, like an obstinate child in the arms of its mother, by what God has determined and done for his salvation in spite of his own opposition."[11] Barth is speaking of revelation not on the grounds of comparative religions, nor from a phenomenological point of view, but strictly in light of Christ (*sub specie Christi*). The reasoning is clear: If religions contain the power of salvation, there is no need for Christ. If religion reveals God, what is the use of Christ? Because the religions claim to do what God has already done for the world in Christ, they become rivals and an abomination to God. These may be harsh judgments, but they are strictly to be measured by God's revelation in Christ. From a human point of view, Barth admits that there is a lot of good in the religions, and that Christians have no reason to indulge themselves in negative value judgments. Barth, however, is not speaking from a religious point of view but from a revelational one.

If religion cannot reach up to revelation, revelation can reach down to religion. In a kind of Hegelian dialectic, the event of revelation at first spells the *Aufhebung* of religion—the abolition, the negation, or the antithesis of religion—but moves in the second instance to an assumption of religion. The movement of revelation does not end with the destruction of religion but with its elevation. In other words, religion, like the sinner, can be justified. It stands under the divine condemnation; however, that is not the ultimate but only the penultimate word of God. The dark side of Barth's evaluation of the religions is followed by a brighter side. The negative stroke is not the last word, and those who interpret Barth as finally negative have misunderstood him. Religion in the end is positively affirmed, not on the basis of its own pride and glory but solely on account of the light of revelation that shines upon it. Religion is *assumed into* the revelatory event of Jesus Christ, and the justification of religion can take place only within the reality of Jesus Christ. Religion cannot justify itself. Religion is related to revelation as Christ's human nature is related to the divine nature—within the scheme of the incarnation, the assumption of flesh (*assumptio carnis*). There can be no question about it. Barth offers a positive evaluation of religion and the religions, but strictly on the basis of the incarnation.

Wherever the world of the religions hears and obeys the Word of God in Christ, there we have the origin of authentic Christianity. Barth calls Christianity the true religion, not because it is intrinsically better than any other religion but only because it is the place that points to Christ. Christianity is the true religion only by the grace of God and by the name of Jesus Christ. The only real difference between Christianity and other religions is Christ, not any quality in the Christian religion as compared to other religions. Christianity of itself is equally as impotent as other religions in conveying the revelation of God. It lives exclusively by the grace of God in Jesus Christ.

In the last volume of *Church Dogmatics,* Barth utters his final evaluation about the world of the non-Christian religions. His tone is subdued and expansive, and the harsh judgments of the early Barth are mostly missing. One does not need to hypothesize that Barth has changed his mind or contradicted himself, only that he is looking more at the positive side of the dialectic. In volume four of *Church Dogmatics,* Barth turns again to the topic of the world religions under the rubric of the prophetic office of Christ. His leading proposition in this section is verbatim the first article of the Barmen Declaration: "Jesus Christ as attested to us in Holy Scripture is the one Word of God whom we must hear and whom we must trust and obey in life and in death."[12] The exclusive uniqueness of Christ as the sole mediator between God and the world is reaffirmed in continuity with his earlier period. If, in the earlier period, Barth had his eye on the divinity of God, the starting point of the incarnation, in his later period he turned his attention more to the humanity of God, the actual occurrence of the incarnation in the world.

Barth never compromised his christocentric thesis that Jesus Christ is the one and only light that brings life to the world. He was aware, however, of all the pressures in modern theology that could compromise this thesis; for example, consider the intellectual reproach that complains that the Barmen confession of *solus Christus* "fosters a sorry restriction of the field of vision of human knowledge." A scientific theology for the modern age may find the christological clause obscurantist. Consider both the moral accusation that the clause arrogantly "leads to the breakdown of communication . . . even in the last resort of fellowship between Christians and non-Christians"[13] and the political accusation that christocentric revelation breeds intolerance "with all the accompanying horrors of burnings, religious wars, crusades and similar procedures." All of these charges tempt a sensitive Christian "either to suppress the statement altogether or to render it so innocuous that it no longer says what it purports to say."[14] Barth was writing these words in the 1960s. They are even more applicable today when the shibboleths of pluralism and relativism are the twin towers of the more recent theology of Babel.

Barth says that these reproaches against his christological thesis can be partly softened by removing a common misunderstanding: "The statement that Jesus Christ is the one Word of God has really nothing whatever to do with the arbitrary exaltation and self-glorification of the Christian in relation to other men, of the Church in relation to other institutions, or of Christianity in relation to other conceptions." In other words, the centrality of Christ in divine revelation does not justify the "intention of absolutising our own Christian subjectivity or that of the Church and its tradition."[15] In making the christological confession, the church is not to exalt or glorify itself at the expense of others. The church is not speaking on its own authority but is pointing in the direction of the scriptural witness to the unique authority of Jesus Christ. From the very beginning, the message of Jesus Christ has entered the world alongside a "multiplicity of religious, cultic and doctrinal systems."[16] Pluralism is nothing new; neither is the awareness of this phenomenon. Israel and Christianity have always been surrounded by "other nations with other histories, religions, pieties, orders and divinities."[17] The biblical prophets, evangelists, and apostles knew all about these facts; and they proclaimed the Lordship of God in the face of all the publics that can possibly exist, not only in the sphere of private religion.

Barth then goes on to make an assertion that explodes the usual caricatures of his theology. He asserts:

> We recognize that the fact that Jesus Christ is the one Word of God does not mean that in the Bible, the Church and the world there are not other words which are quite notable in their way, other lights which are quite clear and other revelations which are quite real. . . . Nor does it follow from our statement that every word spoken outside the circle of the Bible and the Church is a word of false prophecy and therefore valueless, empty and corrupt, that all the lights which rise and shine in this outer sphere are misleading and all the revelations are necessarily untrue.[18]

What does Barth mean to say? He means to say that "Jesus Christ is the one and only Word of God, that He alone is the light of God and the revelation of God." He also says, however, that, in the service of that Word, there are other words that point to it and that such words are not only found in the Bible or the church. He says: "Nor is it impossible that words of this kind should be uttered outside this circle if the whole world of creation and history is the realm of the lordship of the God at whose right hand Jesus Christ is seated, so that he exercises authority in this outer as well as the inner sphere and is free to attest Himself or to cause Himself to be attested in it."[19]

Barth has usually been known to restrict the witness to the Word of God in Jesus Christ to the Bible and the church. Now he clearly speaks of another circle of witnesses, including words and signs and lights and revelations in the world of non-Christian religions, apart from and not dependent on the Bible or the Church. Barth's christological thesis is not shaken by this acknowledgment of a third circle of witnesses beyond the Bible and the church. None of them can replace or supplement the one Word of God in Jesus Christ. Jesus Christ is not the only word; he is the only Word of God as good as God is, who has the authority and power of God. All other words and witnesses outside the wall of the church (*extra muros ecclesiae*) must be measured by this one Word of God in Jesus Christ; and yet Barth is sincere about these extramural words of other religions and systems, including modern neopaganism and secular humanism.

What is the relation between the one Word of God in Jesus Christ and the true and good words spoken outside the pages of the Bible and beyond the walls of the church? Barth calls them "parables of the kingdom."[20] The community that has been commissioned to proclaim Jesus Christ as the one and only Word of God must accept the fact that there are such parables of the kingdom in the world outside the Bible and the church and that they are saying materially the same thing, "although from a different source and in another tongue."[21] The community must listen to these alien witnesses to the truth, search for material agreement, and let them illumine, accentuate, and explain (without replacing or rivaling) the biblical and Christian witnesses.

How is it possible that the eternal Word of God can be heard in the words of other religions out of touch with the Bible and the church? Again, for Barth, the answer is a christological one. The risen Christ rules at the right hand of the Father. The sphere of his dominion is not limited to the Bible and the church, to their prophecy and apostolate. It extends beyond the scope of the kerygma, dogma, worship, mission, and entire life of the community in line with the apostles. The whole creation and all people are related to the reconciliation of the world by God through Christ, who is able to speak, to be heard, and to be spoken about outside the walls of the church.

To explain how this is possible, Barth sticks to basic Christology and rejects the way of natural theology. He explains that the parables of the kingdom in other religions and in the secular world are the work of the one sovereign Lord attested by the Bible and the church, whereas natural theology is always in search of an idea of God apart from Christ. Natural theology always relies on the capacity of human reason to reach truth about God; but Barth counts on the capacity of Jesus Christ to create human witnesses wherever he pleases, even against their knowledge and will, and certainly beyond the limits of the Bible and the church. Barth says that "our present contention is that what was and is possible for Him in the narrow sphere is well within His powers in the wider."[22]

Did Barth Teach Universal Salvation?

I have now reached the point where the question is bound to be asked: if the sovereign Christ can reach the world with his word apart from the prophetic, apostolic, and missionary words of the Bible and the church, then in the end will all be saved? Does Barth teach universal salvation? Barth thinks that Christians have taken human unbelief and godlessness too seriously. For the most part, Christians have been too skeptical, pessimistic, and humorless. Barth says that "we are summoned to believe in Him, and in His victorious power, not in the invincibility of any non-Christian, anti-Christian, or pseudo-Christian worldliness which confronts Him. The more seriously and joyfully we believe in Him, the more we shall see such signs in the worldly sphere, and the more we shall be able to receive true words from it."[23]

When we deal with Barth's Christocentrism, the liberals become nervous; and when we deal with Barth's universalism, the conservative evangelicals protest. How can Barth have his cake and eat it too? Having developed the most complex and thoroughgoing Christology in the history of the church, Barth is not able to restrict the confidence born of hope and prayer that God will in the end get his wish that all be saved. In Barth's own words:

> There is no good reason why we should forbid ourselves, or be forbidden, openness to the possibility that in the reality of God and man in Jesus Christ there is contained much more than we might expect and therefore the supremely unexpected withdrawal of that final threat, i.e., that in the truth of this reality there might be contained the super-abundant promise of the final deliverance of all men. To be more explicit, there is no good reason why we should not be open to this possibility . . . of an *apokatastasis* or universal reconciliation.[24]

Barth's universalism is highly nuanced and qualified. It is not a dogma, not a piece of knowledge, and not something to which humans have a right to claim. We may, however, cautiously and distinctly pray and hope that in spite of everything that seems to point conclusively in the opposite direction, God's mercy will not cast off his world forever. Two alternatives to a christocentric universalism are Arminianism and Calvinist double predestination. Barth is closest to the Lutheran doctrine of single predestination, but he draws out some implications from which Lutherans have traditionally recoiled. Those who come to faith in Jesus Christ are elected through God's grace and love. God's justice and wrath have already taken their toll in the rejection of Jesus Christ on the cross. God's love is not limited. It is not limited by human freedom or by divine wrath.

Barth is not a universalist of the unitarian kind. People are not too good to be damned. God need not save everybody nor reject anyone, because God is not bound by anything outside of his will. He is not bound to give the devil his due. If we take into account God's love, we know he would have all to be saved. If we reckon with his freedom, we know he has the power to save whomsoever he pleases. This does not lead to a dogmatic universalism; but it does mean that we leave open the possibility that, within the power of God's freedom and love, all people may indeed be saved in the end. This follows as a possibility from the fact that God is free from all external factors in making up his mind. Not even the human predicament, the need for salvation, is the primary motive of God's love in Jesus Christ. God loves because it is his nature to love, not first because there are people in need of his love.

The other side of the possibility of universal salvation is that of reprobation. We cannot rule out the possibility of divine reprobation to those who remain in unbelief and disobedience to the end. If reprobation is a possibility in principle that cannot be ruled out, then the threat of eternal rejection is seen in a new light at the moment one contemplates the atonement of Jesus Christ. The threat of eternal condemnation is real for all people, but God will not necessarily actualize this possibility. Christians may hope and pray that all might be saved and that the distinction between those who already believe and those who do not yet believe will ultimately be destroyed by the Word of God who "is able from these stones to raise up children to Abraham" (Matt 3:9).

The scale tilts decidedly toward the hope of universal reconciliation on account of Christ. It cannot be denied that eternal reprobation is a possibility; but in the light of God's verdict in the victory of Jesus Christ, it becomes an "impossible possibility." Barth says:

> No aversion, rebellion or resistance on the part of non-Christians will be strong enough to resist the fulfillment of the promise of the Spirit which is pronounced over them too . . . or to hinder the overthrow of their ignorance in the knowledge of Jesus Christ [because] the stream is too strong and the dam too weak for us to be

able reasonably to expect anything but the collapse of the dam and the onrush of the waters. In this sense Jesus Christ is the hope even of these non-Christians.[25]

In a still more explicit passage, Barth states that the justification of the world of sinners in Jesus Christ is the content of predestination: "The exchange which took place on Golgotha, when God chose as his throne the malefactor's cross, when the Son of God bore what the son of man ought to have borne, took place once and for all in fulfillment of God's eternal will, and it can never be reversed. There is no condemnation—literally none—for those that are in Christ Jesus."[26] Then he says, more boldly still, that after the coming of Jesus Christ, unbelief becomes "an objective, real, ontological impossibility. . . . Faith, however, has become an objective, real ontological inevitability for all, for every man."[27]

This chapter contains only a small sample of Barth's rich theological legacy to us. In his many books and volumes on dogmatics, however, Barth devotes to the world only a very limited number of pages. Barth did not have any profound firsthand experience of life in the context of other religions. What he learned about them came out of books from the safe distance of a library in Switzerland, but he has shown that the way to develop a Christian theology of hope for the world religions is through the word of divine revelation in Jesus Christ. Barth did not say the last word on this subject, and most of what he did say has been ignored, particularly by the specialists in the field of the world religions. I believe the time has come to take another look at Barth's christocentric approach, but first some of the negative caricatures of his theology must be removed from prejudicial thinking of many modern Protestant and progressive Catholic theologians.

Thomas Torrance once referred to Karl Barth as "the great Church father of Protestant Christendom, the one genuine doctor of the Protestant Church the modern era has known." I believe that his day is still to come in the United States, perhaps after some decades of drift into the quagmire of neopaganism that American Christianity seems to be heading. Barthianism certainly worked in the struggles of the 1930s, and it might work again.

Although I cannot count myself a Barthian and have often been numbered among his Lutheran critics, I have been listening again to the voice of Barth at the point where I find his greatest strength: his concentration on Christ as the heart of the church's message and mission, particularly in a time when the church is dissolving itself into what Barth called *Kulturprotestantismus* (cultural Protestantism).

[4]

Christ Is God's Final, Not the Only, Revelation

ARNOLD TOYNBEE ended his *Christianity among the Religions of the World* with a story about an incident that happened when Christian Rome was forcibly closing the pagan temples and suppressing pagan forms of worship. The government ordered the removal of the statue of Victory from the senate house at Rome, which had been placed there by Julius Caesar. The spokesman of the senate at the time was Quintus Aurelius Symmachus, who had a controversy on the subject with St. Ambrose. In one of his last pleas, Symmachus put into the record these words: "It is impossible that so great a mystery should be approached by one road only."[1] Toynbee concludes his story with his own counsel: "The mystery of which he is speaking is the mystery of the Universe, the mystery of Man's encounter with God, the mystery of God's relation to good and evil. Christianity has never answered Symmachus. To suppress a rival religion is not an answer. The question raised by Symmachus is still alive in the World today. I think we shall have to face it in our time."[2]

Toynbee's story tells us about one approach to religious pluralism: Rub it out; and use force if necessary, which is just what the age of Christendom did! About a thousand years later, Nicholas of Cusa, a Cardinal and member of the Papal Court, wrote *De Pace Fidei,* which called for the opposite approach to religious pluralism: Let there be peace among the different forms of faith! He imagines a heavenly conversation between members

65

of the various religions when the divine Logos explains their unity. "There is only one religion, only one cult of all who are living according to the principles of Reason [the Logos-Reason], which underlies the different rites. . . . The cult of the gods everywhere witnesses to Divinity. . . . So in the heaven of [Logos-Reason] the concord of the religions was established."[3] The Cardinal of Cusa wrote his book when the crusading spirit was still strong in the church, and he anticipated the spirit of tolerance championed by the philosophers of the Enlightenment.

In the twentieth century, we receive yet another idea that views the many religions as intrinsically the same. John Hick calls for "a Copernican revolution in our thinking about Christianity and the religions."[4] In contrast to the old Ptolemaic astronomy in which the earth is the center of the solar system, with all the other heavenly bodies revolving around it, Hick thinks we need to catch up to the Copernican view, which shifts the center from the earth to the sun. By analogy then, the traditional idea that Christ and, therefore, Christianity lie at the center of all the religions is as outdated as the geocentric Ptolemaic theory. The Copernican view would place God and not Christ at the center, with Christianity and all the religions revolving around it.

To continue to be christocentric today is about as anachronistic as to believe that the earth is flat. The image is persuasive. No one wants to be accused of being so unmodern, unscientific, and uneducated as to believe that anymore. According to Hick's Copernican revolution, the price we have to pay to be truly theocentric in an age of religious pluralism is to give up all the exclusive particles of Christology and the gospel which they modify, to give up all references to Christ or the gospel as the one and only way, truth, and life, the one and only name or power of God unto salvation, the one and only Lord, Savior, and Son of God, the one and only incarnate Word, mediator, and sacrifice who reconciles the world unto the Father. In order to overcome every negative aspect of Christian exclusiveness that has allegedly spawned a combination of nasty attitudes and actions—intolerance, arrogance, superiority, triumphalism, colonialism, crusades, inquisition, pogroms, anti-Semitism, apartheid, genocide, and the like—the axe is laid at the root and source of all such evil: the New Testament's picture and preaching that Jesus Christ is somehow unique, universal, final, and normative, as expressed in terms of a wide variety of symbols and titles of honor.

I have noted two responses to the challenge of religious pluralism. The response of imperial Christianity was to squash the pluralism, and that led to the age of Christendom ruled by force. Such an approach, however, is heteronomous and authoritarian, and it ill befits the gospel and the kingdom it announces. The second response is antithetical, motivated by the spirit of peace and tolerance under the sway of an enlightened view of reason alone. Such a response, however, is allied with a debilitating skepticism and vacuous relativism that break the very links of Christian identity and apostolic continuity that connect the Christian faith's originating and sustaining events and witnesses.

The Reality of Revelation in the Religions

The basis and starting point of a Lutheran understanding of the world of religions other than Christian is neither primarily nor exclusively the revelation of God in the history of Israel, Jesus, and the church. Luther started what has become a consistent affirmation of a general revelation of God apart from the Bible and the history of salvation culminating in Christ. When we survey contemporary Lutheran theologians from various schools of thought, we find a broad understanding of God's revelation at work in the religions without any necessary historical connection with the Bible and the Christian tradition. This is true with respect to such dissimilar Lutheran theologians as Nathan Söderblom, Paul Tillich, Paul Althaus, Carl Heinz Ratschow, Gustaf Wingren, and Wolfhart Pannenberg. They have all successfully withstood Karl Barth's christocentric reduction of the doctrine of revelation. The first article of the creed witnesses to God the Creator of all things, and this witness comes prior to the confession of Christ in the second article who came "for us and our salvation." We find in the religions an echo of God's activity in all expressions of life because God has not left himself without a witness among the nations (Acts 14:16-17), which means that the reality of God and his revelation

67

lie behind the religions of humanity as anonymous mystery and hidden power. Lutheran theology typically affirms a twofold revelation of God: through the hidden God of creation and law (*Deus absconditus*) and through the revealed God of covenant and gospel (*Deus revelatus*). Lutheran theologians use different terms in making this distinction, but they agree in opposing a christo-monopolistic doctrine of revelation.

Personal experience of God's revelation is happening in the religions everywhere. The religions owe their life to the ongoing activity of God, and God works in contrasting ways in the world. The way of Christ is one of them, but another way is revealed in the religions. Christian theology views the religions as bearing their own special witness to God's ongoing activity in the world and through the many dimensions of law which upholds order in society. God is active through the structures of common human experience, and God is universally experienced in all the religions as a pressure that drives people to seek what is right and just and good and true. In Luther's language, this pressure may be viewed as the work of God's left hand, and people receive many gifts from this hand. Under the pressure of God's activity, people are bound to respond; and religion is the dimension through which this response is channeled. God is behind the quest for God, and the religions are full of stories of people setting out in search of truth and the meaning of both their own existence and all reality. Augustine's dictum is true: "Thou hast made us for thyself, and our hearts are restless until they find their rest in thee."

One strategy that Lutherans are wise to refuse is to join forces with those who hold an illusionistic theory of religion. In the interest of stressing the *solus Christus,* some have made common cause with the atheistic critique of religion, which holds that religion is only a projection, an illusion or opiate generated out of human need and fantasy. After the atheistic critique has freed humankind from the religions, then presumably we will be able to proclaim the message of Christ to an eagerly awaiting world—a fatal maneuver, because in exorcising one demon, seven more rush in to take its place. Barth is well known for having used Feuerbach to make way for his theology of revelation against the approach of the history-of-religions school, Troeltsch and company. To the contrary, I want to emphasize that God is at work in the religions to bring forth witness to himself. When we read the sacred writings of the various religions, we can perceive voices pointing to the revelation of God's power and glory.

This view of the religions is not a systematic theological postulate dangling in the air but one based on an appeal to biblical exegesis and church tradition. The New Testament nowhere makes the claim that Christ is the one and only revelation of God in history and to humanity. The presupposition of the gospel message is that God has already spoken his Word, that people already encounter God and know him in some way apart from the biblical witness. In Rom 1:18-32, Paul clearly affirms a divine revelation prior to and apart from the gospel of salvation in Jesus Christ. I do not speak here of a natural theology in the sense of medieval scholasticism, but I hold that divine revelation is taking place through the visible reality of the creation and human experience. Lutherans are not prepared to say that we can perceive the human face of God in this way, but we can know something of God—as Luther would put it, the *posteriora Dei* (the hind parts of God). To be sure, Paul's argument was not to affirm a true knowledge of God in the religions for its own sake; it was to assert a *praeparatio evangelica* (preparation for the gospel) showing that people are under the wrath and judgment of God, steeped in guilt and lies, and in need of the gospel and its redemption.

In Romans 2 and 7 Paul speaks of the law written on the hearts of the Gentiles, which is nothing else than the law of God working universally through the conscience of people who know not Christ. Although the understanding of this law may be dark and confusing apart from Christ, its fundamental content is the same as the law given to Israel, in relation to which Christ is announced as its end and fulfillment. From this point, Lutherans have been able to spell out some analogies. Just as the church fathers could say that Greek philosophy was a preamble to the gospel analogous to the function of Jewish law, so also the religions may play a similar role in the history of humanity. Every religion has prophets who are similar to John the Baptist preparing the way for the coming of Christ. If this were not so, the gospel of Christ would drop like a stone from heaven and could not be translated into other religiocultural settings.

The prologue of the Gospel of John refers to the Logos who is the source of light and life of all people. This Logos is the principle of universal enlightenment of all people in all times, so that truth, wherever it may be found, will function in the end as a witness to the truth of God incarnate. The same Logos who is the medium of creation is also a medium of salvation. Of course, the crucial point of John's prologue lies in the dark words that undergird the necessity of Christ and the preaching of the gospel: "Yet the world did not know him. . . . and his own people did not accept him" (1:10-11).

I have given some samples of the kind of biblical interpretation that open Lutherans to an acceptance of the reality of God and his revelation in the religions, but this approach is also borne out in the history of the Christian tradition. The church fathers referred to the "seeds of the logos" scattered through the philosophy of the Greeks and the mysteries of religion. Also, the theologians of Lutheran orthodoxy wrote lengthy treatises on general revelation; but what about Luther himself? Luther no doubt believed there was valid albeit partial knowledge of God apart from the biblical revelation of the Word and faith. Luther held that, both according to the witness of Scripture and by looking at the religions, we can believe that people have a certain amount of knowledge concerning divine things. For Luther, however, that was not enough, not enough to grasp God's final will and testament for humanity and its ultimate future destiny. The true and proper knowledge of God comes only through the revelation of Christ. Lutheran orthodoxy clearly taught a twofold revelation and knowledge of God: the general revelation of God through creation and law, and the special revelation of God through Christ and the gospel.

On the basis of this general affirmation of the revelation of God in the religions, how explicit and positive can Lutherans be about the value and meaning of the non-Christian religious world? Many Lutherans would respond in the negative because they hold the completely negative view that the religions offer people a one-way ticket bound for hell. This verdict, however, is not generally supported by those Lutheran theologians who have thought long and hard about the significance of the religions in the economy of divine revelation and salvation.

If we examine the theologies of Söderblom, Althaus, Ratschow, Tillich, and Pannenberg, we will find a twentieth-century theology of the religions that integrates them into the history of revelation linked to the eschatological event of Jesus

Christ. As religions they may not mean everything that God intends for the world, but also they do not mean nothing. To ignore the religions would be to sever a portion of God's dealings with human history and the world. The history of religions thus becomes for these Lutheran theologians data for Christian theological reflection.

For Christian theology, the religions cannot establish their meaning in a final way apart from the light that falls on them from the gospel: that is, we know what we know about what God is doing in them in the light of Christ; otherwise, we would not know what sense to make of them. Some definite perspective needs to guide our interpretations and appropriations. Consider, for example, driving down the expressway at night. There are signs by the roadside that objectively make sense, but we cannot read them until our headlights shine upon them. Then we are able to read what they say. So also when the light of Christ shines upon the religions, no longer do they remain in darkness from our perspective, but we see meaning there. Only in the missionary encounters of the religions does this meaning come to light; otherwise, we are dealing with mere hypotheses from the science of religions that swim in the sea of relativity.

For Lutherans today, the new shape of natural theology may well take the form of a theology of the history of religions. It functions as a prolegomenon to a specifically Christian theology of the history of salvation recorded in the Old and New Testaments. Althaus, Ratschow, Tillich, and Pannenberg have called precisely for this approach; and they have warned against the tendency to begin and end theology within the Christian *koinōnia* in which Christians are only speaking Christianese to Christians. We should aim to take seriously all that human beings have experienced and believed about God prior to and apart from the preaching of the gospel. Some argue that this concession to the revelatory quality of the religions detracts from the sole efficacy of Christ in communicating divine revelation. The answer to this fear is that the uniqueness of Christ's role is not limited to revelation but comes to its decisive and definitive expression in the area of justification and reconciliation. Revelation and salvation are not coterminous.

Further, the image of God in human being has not been destroyed; and here we have a point of contact for the notion that God is universally at work in the religions. The fact that God elected to work within the history of Israel in a special way does not mean that God cut off his other activity among the nations. On the contrary, what he was doing with the elect of Israel had representative function in relation to all nations so that, in the end, world history and salvation history are eschatologically unified in the mystery of Christ. The Lord of the church is thus the Savior of the world, and the Savior of the church is the Lord of the world—inseparably. The doctrine of the fall and sin does not obliterate the self-transcending orientation of all people to the Creator, whose eschatological rule is announced in the coming of Christ. Despite sin, there remains a quest for reunion with the God from whom all humans have become estranged, a quest which itself is a sign of the continuing activity of God in his world. We can thus affirm that the history of religions lies within the orbit of God's revelation to the world.

We should avoid making any sweeping judgments about what can be known of God in the world religions apart from his self-revelation in Israel, Jesus, and the church. Paul Althaus rightly points out that Luther believed that the non-Christian religions "can say very many things about the essence of deity and even about its personal being."[5] In light of today's vastly increased knowledge of the religions, however, Christian theology would need to establish this point of view in each particular case. On the basis of the idea of revelation in the religions, for instance, Christian theology would be open to a positive evaluation of the so-called religions of grace, Bhakti Hinduism and Mahayana Buddhism. These religions seem to move beyond the limits of either mysticism or moralism and to view the relationship between God and humanity solely on the basis of grace; that is, humans do not have the ability to do anything for their salvation, but they are radically dependent on the reality of divine saving grace. Humans are too weak or limited to be able to reach God by the way of works or knowledge. This view corresponds to the doctrine of *sola gratia* and is actually a principle of *sola fide*. Analogous to the Lutheran view, this faith is not conceived as a work or a condition that humans can achieve to merit salvation. Francis Xavier identified the Jodo Shinshu as "the Lutheran form of Buddhism" because it relied solely on Amida's grace and not on personal works. Lutheran theologians such as Althaus and Tillich have referred to these religions as examples of a real knowledge of God apart from the Christian revelation. The Lutheran missionary R. L. Reichelt tried to implement this notion of general revelation on the mission field. He believed that if ever there was a true revelation of God apart from Christ, it would be here in the belief that the merciful and loving God is willing to take the despised and rejected sinners unto himself. Can we not conclude, therefore, on the basis of such religio-historical findings, that there are preparations for the Christian gospel in certain historical forms of religion even though they might fall short of the full revelation of God in the personal sacrifice and cross of Jesus Christ?

Perhaps we can say about these religions of grace what Jesus said to the scribe in Mark 12:34: "You are not far from the Kingdom of God." Karl Barth was saying much the same thing by his notion of the parables of the kingdom outside the pages of the Bible and beyond the walls of the church.[6] This third circle of witnesses includes words and signs and lights and revelations in the world of the religions independent of the Bible and the church that say materially the same thing, "although from a different source and in another tongue."[7] How this is possible is for Barth a further sign of the Lordship of Christ who has the power to create witnesses to the kingdom whenever he pleases, not only in the narrow sphere but in the wider sphere as well. If Barth approached this notion cautiously and late in his life (to the surprise of many of his critics), Lutheran theologians had been asserting this sort of thing all along on the grounds of God's twofold way of working in the world, through the universal law of creation (*lex creationis*) and the particular gospel of salvation in Christ.

The Gospel of Salvation and the Religions

Now I must turn to a highly controversial issue in current thinking about Christianity and the religions: whether the religions are ways of salvation. We have acknowledged that God brings forth witnesses to his power and glory within the religions, clearly taught in Scripture; but the question is whether God also uses them as ways of salvation—a new doctrine taught by some progressive Catholic theologians, who build on Karl

Rahner's notions of the "supernatural existential" and "anonymous Christianity," as well as by some liberal Protestant theologians, who approach the issue chiefly from the history and phenomenology of religions. My task here is to explore what Lutheran theology says about the gospel of salvation and the religions, and why.

Again my approach is typological. I am asking what Lutheran theologians—Söderblom, Althaus, Tillich, Ratschow, Pannenberg—have to say on the subject rather than exploring their conceptual and convictional differences in detail. I agree with the overall judgment of Paul Knitter regarding the typically Lutheran answer to the question about salvation in the religions. He makes it a point of criticism that Lutherans show an inability to admit true, full, and equal salvation in the religions because of their belief in the salvific centrality of the gospel and Christ.[8] Although they may know the empirical data of the history of religions, Lutherans stick to the Reformation insight concerning salvation "by faith alone" resting on "Christ alone." Knitter is quite right; Lutherans typically insist on the necessity of Christ both ontologically and epistemologically in their construction of a theology of the religions. For Lutherans, Christ is not merely *expressive* of a divine salvation equally available in the plurality of religions; salvation is *constituted* by the coming of God in the concrete history of Jesus of Nazareth. A Logos Christology reaching universality without its particular basis and content in the historical Jesus is docetic and void of the gospel.

In Lutheran theology the gospel of Christ functions as the final medium of revelation and therefore the critical norm in a theology of the history of religions. Whatever may be phenomenologically described as revelatory experiences in the religions, Christian theology defines salvation on the model of what God has accomplished for the world and humanity in the life, death, and resurrection of Jesus, the Christ. So Althaus says: "Outside of Christ there is indeed a self-manifestation of God, and therefore knowledge of God, but it does not lead to salvation, to union between God and man."[9] Carl Heinz Ratschow finds a "total and central distinction"[10] between the gospel and the religions in spite of many striking parallels between Christianity and non-Christian faiths. The doctrine of justification points to an understanding of salvation that ultimately constitutes a "deep and fundamental difference" that is finally nothing less than an "absolute antithesis."[11] The only explanation for drawing such a clear line of distinction between Christianity and the religions lies in the *solus Christus*. For Paul Tillich, the new being in Jesus as the Christ is the criterion not only of Christianity but of the history of religions, because what happened in Jesus Christ makes him the center of all revelation and of all history. Wolfhart Pannenberg binds God's final revelation at the end of time to the history of Jesus as its proleptic medium. Thus he says: "If God is revealed through Jesus Christ, then who or what God is becomes defined only by the Christ event. . . . The essence of God is not accessible at all without Jesus Christ."[12] I could go on to cite innumerable passages from Lutheran theologians past and present to show that when it comes to the understanding of salvation, they are all equally as christocentric as Karl Barth. The reason for this seems obvious. They draw their understanding of the gospel of salvation and its relation to the wide world of religious experience from the standpoint of biblical revelation and Reformation insights. The Scripture principle (*sola Scriptura*) in some way provides a common bond among these theologians.

Although Lutheran theologians have traditionally called justification the *articulus stantis et cadentis ecclesiae,* twentieth-century Lutheran theology has extended its application to a wider theology of culture and the religions. Tillich's Protestant principle provides a contemporary interpretation of justification as the *articulus stantis et cadentis ecclesiae* that judges the religions, including Christianity as a religion. All religions fall short as ways of salvation, including all their mystical and moralistic attempts at self-elevation to the level of God. Anders Nygren referred to these as the ways of *nomos* religion and *erōs* religion, insights he derived critically from an *agapē* (altruistic) perspective which pictures God in the self-condescending act of justifying sinners in Christ. The word of the cross, from Luther to Kähler to Althaus and Tillich, becomes the critical norm to interpret the world of religions.

Justification *sola fide* cuts the root of human pride and self-divinization in order to let God be God. Faith alone allows God alone to do the work of salvation; the religions try to achieve salvation through human works. As Ratschow puts it: "In Christianity the human role in salvation is consecutive; in the religions it is constitutive."[13] To view the religions *sub specie justificationis* (in light of justification) means that just as the Creator could create all things out of nothing, so he can also exchange life for death, peace for enmity, and righteousness for sin. Faith must be *sola* because sin negates every human capacity to do something on the basis of which to make things right with God. To convert the *sola* into a kind of synergy or synthesis of divine and human action leading to justification destroys the whole process of salvation. Religions are not able to escape from this radical state of sinfulness, so they are often the place where humans intensify their rebellion and seek to hide from the judgment of God. Sin is basically the lack of the ability to live *sola fide* before God and is, therefore, the primal wrong against the divinity of God, the very first commandment, from which the others follow. There is an inner drive in all humanity against God, and every religion is permeated by this condition. No religion, therefore, is capable of generating the freedom to let God be God, which only faith can do.

Luther's concept of the bondage of will comes into play in assessing the relation between the gospel and religion. Sin, the lack of faith and freedom, correlates with the negative aspects of God's revelation to humanity. Sinners stand condemned under the wrath and judgment of God, and God becomes the enemy. We are commanded to love our enemy with all our heart and mind and soul, and this demand can even drive us more deeply into rebellion and fanatical religious activity. Religions can be used as a shield or shelter from the just and angry Judge and offer cheap grace and the promise of salvation in exchange for fulfilling their demands, and demands of religion are always negotiable and conditional. The religions know what we must do for our salvation, and we are happy to oblige because they exact a price we can pay. Thus the religions themselves fall under the wrath and judgment of God despite all the good and truth that they also undeniably have given to human experience and history.

The gospel opens the door to reconciliation with God at the same time that it closes the other doors of self-salvation through works of the law, mystical exercises, or metaphysical gnosis. The *solus Christus* provides the basis and content establishing the *sola fide*. At one point in history God has communicated his reconciling love to and for the world—in the death and resurrection of Jesus Christ. Why is Christ necessary to mend the broken relationship between God and humanity? We can offer no a priori kind of reason whose validity can be demonstrated independently of the fact that this is the way it actually happened. It is characteristic of a Lutheran theology of the gospel to begin its soteriology with the actuality of the God-in-Christ occurrence and then proceed to search for its deeper meaning and foundation in the doctrines of election and eschatology. Some Lutheran theologians go far in speculating about the eternal presuppositions and the eschatological implications of the gospel; others stay close to the exegetical ground of the doctrine of the gospel. They all start "from below," however, with the givens of the gospel, and they then probe how the necessity of Christ for the salvation of the world may be best understood.

Gerhard Forde's various writings on the atonement and justification show that there is no uniform interpretive theory in the history of Lutheranism, nor is there scholarly consensus about Luther's own scheme. They all do, however, share a solid core where Christ stands as the essential representative between God and humanity, representing God for the world and the world before God. I cannot here go into the various theories and motifs Lutheran theologians have used to explain why Jesus Christ must be truly God and truly man (*vere Deus et vere homo*) in the light of soteriology. There is even disagreement between Tillich and Pannenberg on the relation between Christology and soteriology. Tillich asserts that "Christology is a function of soteriology," and Pannenberg says it's the other way around. Whatever the theoretical differences, however, somehow Christ is the place where the contradiction between God and humanity gets resolved—actually and necessarily. In this one person, Jesus Christ—through his life, ministry, death, and resurrection— salvation is effected for the world through the outpouring of the love of God, who overcomes his wrath and enables the "happy exchange" to take place. Christ does not merely tell the world of God's love; he makes it happen by reconciling God and the world to each other. Something actually has to happen as the necessary condition and efficient cause of salvation, and the locus of this happening is Christ alone.

On the basis of salvation through Christ alone and justification by faith alone, Lutheran theology has no certain grounds for teaching that the religions as such are ways of salvation and that people are saved through whatever the religion into which they happen to be born. Outside of Christ and apart from the preaching of the gospel there are no known historical alternatives that may be theologically accepted as divinely authorized means of salvation. If traditionally Roman Catholic theology taught that "outside the church there is no salvation," Lutheran theology has taught that "outside of Christ there is no salvation." Finally, the only unique thing that Christianity has to offer the world is its witness to Christ; and by Christ we do not mean some anonymous Christ principle but the concrete reality and historical person of Jesus as the Christ. When Raimundo Panikkar writes that Christ has other names—Rama, Krishna, Isvara, Purusha, Tathagata, and the like—we must disagree mightily.[14] Panikkar's universal Christ who goes by many names is parallel to John Hick's universal God who has as many names as all the religions in the world have bestowed on him, and they are supposedly all equally valid. These theologians are jumping directly from phenomenological facts to theological judgments without benefit of the kind of christological critique that a trinitarian theology of the cross would require.

Lutheran theology has consistently affirmed that the real historical Christ mediates himself through Word and sacraments in the power of the Spirit. Just as the objective vertical rift between God and humanity is overcome in the concrete history of Jesus Christ, so also the subjective horizontal distance between the *ephapax* (once-for-all event) of that history and all subsequent times is bridged by the hermeneutical channels of the Word (as both audible and visible words) that creates and perpetuates the church and sends it on its world-historical mission to the nations. Paul says in Rom 10:14: "But how are they to call on one in whom they have not believed? And how are they to believe in one of whom they have never heard? And how are they to hear without someone to proclaim him?" The redeeming presence of the historical Christ must be communicated through the preaching of the Word and the administration of the sacraments. We simply have no certain knowledge about how the same salvation might be communicated apart from the Word and faith. The church, therefore, is under orders to follow through in mediating to the nations an explicit encounter with the historical Christ through words and deeds that witness to his salvific significance.

The Eschatological Proviso

Does the Lutheran insistence on the particularity of the gospel mean that God's universal will unto salvation will be frustrated in the end? In short, do Lutherans teach universal salvation— that all persons whom God would have to be saved will be saved in the end? Lutherans do not in fact agree on the eschatological outcome of God's mission to the nations. Some take an incredibly pessimistic view that only a handful of faithful will escape the holocaust of Sodom and Gomorrah and that all the moral and immoral majority will go to hell. Others follow the trajectory of hope and count on eschatological effects of Christ's historical redemption, so that the salvation now being worked out *in* history will in the end be realized as the salvation *of* history.

This eschatological proviso is a relatively new note that has been struck within a Lutheran theology of the religions. We cannot claim anything like a Lutheran consensus with regard to a systematic theology of the religions constructed from the perspective of eschatology. New insights, however, might be forthcoming from an application of an eschatological perspective. Just as the religions are relativized from the perspective of the gospel, so also Christianity itself is relativized in light of the absolute future of the kingdom it is called to serve. Just as the religions are a preparation for the gospel, which takes particular historical forms, so also the churches are a preparation for the final coming of the kingdom, which will embrace universal historical forms beyond the separation between the church and the world and beyond the separation between Christianity and the religions. This idea emerges out of the conviction that the historical process of which Christianity is a part has universal meaning because of the connection of the eschatological revelation of God in Jesus Christ with the totality of history. Christianity lives and moves and has its being within the universal stream of the religions. The gospel must make its way in this universal historical context, but the final conclusive proof of its power to accomplish the will of God for the salvation of all the nations will come only at the end of history. Meanwhile, as Gustaf Wingren puts it:

> That everyone should be saved is not an assertion of fact that has any biblical support. But it is something one can certainly pray for. . . . No one has arrived. So, while we are in the process of moving toward the goal, we can pray what we cannot assert. For one thing, the New Testament clearly says that God wants everyone to be saved (I Tim. 2:4). To pray for that which God wants is naturally appropriate to the forward movement.[15]

We live in the interim between the particularity of the historical means of salvation and the universality of the vision which the gospel proclaims. Just as Israel made its particular witness in the midst of other religious traditions and assimilated elements of them along the way, so also Christianity has been involved for two thousand years in a process of formation in exchange with other religions. This process will continue, through evangelical outreach and interreligious dialogue. There is no reason to choose between the two forms. Through it all, however, Christian faith is called to do the one thing needful: to witness to the eschatological revelation which Christ brings to the world, in whom the end of all history has appeared as the meaning and future of all the religions. In this way the idea of radical religious pluralism is taken up into the eschatological unity of all reality in the coming of God in the person of Jesus.

The model I am proposing pictures Jesus Christ as the revelation of the eschatological fulfillment of the religions. The gospel of Jesus Christ does not destroy but fulfills the religions. The universality of Christ is something that is being worked out through the interaction of the religions and will be established for all eyes to see only at the end of history. Neither Christianity nor the plurality of religions has arrived at the endpoint of history where Christ will be revealed as the universal future and fulfillment of the totality of nature, history, culture, and religion. We are all together moving forward on this way, aware that we have not yet arrived at the end. In relation to overblown or minimalistic conjectures about how God is working within the religions to orient them to the future of salvation revealed in Christ, we are free to waffle somewhere between reverent speculation and silent agnosticism. This waffling implies that the salvation of those who do not believe in Christ in this lifetime is ultimately a mystery which we cannot unveil by speculation. We can and must, however, say with Paul that we have received the gift of God's grace "to bring to the Gentiles the news of the boundless riches of Christ, and to make everyone see what is the plan of the mystery hidden for ages in God who created all things; so that through the church the wisdom of God in its rich variety might now be made known to the rulers and authorities in the heavenly places. This was in accordance with the eternal purpose that he has carried out in Christ Jesus our Lord" (Eph 3:8-11).

[5]

Christianity Needs a
Theology of Religions

HARVEY COX HAS WRITTEN another best-seller, a timely book reflecting on his personal encounter with people of other faiths. The book's title, *Many Mansions,* is taken from the passage in John's Gospel, "In my Father's house are many mansions: if it were not so, I would have told you" (Authorized Version). This book makes its contribution to the new pluralistic theology that holds that all religions are pretty much equal as ways of salvation. So far as the book has any theology, there is not much with which I can agree. I do think one of his proposals is right, however, and that is the one concerned with the place to start a Christian dialogue with persons of other religions.

Harvey Cox contrasts two poles in the Christian approach to other religions, the universalist and the particularist. The universalist looks for common ground by comparing beliefs and rituals and finally ascending to some ultimate reality or higher essence above and beyond all particulars. You may call it "God" or the "Really Real." If a universalist is a Christian, the strategy is to prefer talk about a "cosmic Christ" to the concrete historical figure of Jesus. There may be something "Christic" about Jesus but not exclusively so, not in a categorically unique way. Harvey Cox confesses that he has sat through many rounds of interfaith dialogues based on one or another version of this universalist model, and he finds it boring, a "tedious exercise" and a "repetitious exchange of vacuities."[1] The strategy of Christian universalism has generally been guilty of "soft-pedaling the figure of Jesus himself."[2]

Harvey Cox recommends that Christians begin with what is of utmost personal passionate interest to them, which is never something abstract and conceptual but, rather, their experience of faith in Jesus Christ. He says, "After all, Jesus is in some ways the *most* particularistic element of Christianity."[3] Cox would clearly distance himself from one kind of particularism, and so would I—the fanaticism that tries to ram Jesus down the throats of other people. That is, however, not the necessary accompaniment of particularism because people of other faiths really want to hear about Jesus. Jesus is much more interesting than some abstract symbol. Cox says that from his experience the Jesus factor is surprisingly just what the non-Christian participants in dialogue are most interested in and most eager to talk about. Cox candidly confesses, "I too tried to avoid talking about Jesus too quickly, but I soon discovered my interlocutors wanted me to."[4]

Which Jesus?

After that point of agreement with Harvey Cox, I come quickly to the parting of the ways because it is not enough simply to talk about Jesus, certainly not any old kind of Jesus. The question is: which Jesus are we talking about? Or whose Jesus are we prepared to call the Lord and Savior? When it comes to talking about Jesus, two ways have been tried over and over again, both of them old-fashioned, but both still much in vogue. The one I will call by its ancient label, the Ebionite Jesus. This approach focuses on "The Life and Teachings of Jesus." Jesus is pictured as a great moral teacher, certainly one of the top ten along with Gautama, Lao Tse, Socrates, Confucius, and Muhammad. Jesus was a rabbi and a prophet and maybe even a mystic; but in the end, after all the superlatives are exhausted, Jesus is a mere man, not more than a man, and that is what the Ebionites old and new believe. At best Jesus can be a model for us, be it his morality, his piety, his life-style, or whatever; the choice is up to us.

The other approach lies at the other end of the christological spectrum. I will call it, using another ancient label, the Docetic Christ. The key concept is the ancient Greek philosophical idea of the Logos. Heraclitus was the first to use this concept philosophically. The Logos is the divine power present in all things.

Seeds of the Logos are sown in the world and make things what they are, accounting for their movement, structure, and meaning. Armed with this knowledge about the universal Logos, acquired through reason and experience, we may apply it to Jesus of Nazareth and call him the Logos, because he expressed or exemplifies this principle in his life and teachings in an eminent way. This Logos principle is the ideal Christ, who does not coincide with the historical Jesus. It is the Logos that saves, and this Logos is universally reflected in all the religions. Jesus bears witness to the Logos, and we can even speak of the incarnation of the Logos in Jesus, but not in a categorically unique way. This type of christological thinking is docetic (from the Greek *dokeō,* to seem) because the concrete history of Jesus is not definitive and constitutive of his Christness.

At bottom there is not that much difference between the ebionitic and docetic approaches. In the end, Jesus is not categorically unique. He is not different from us in essence but only by degree. We are in control of the christological project. The meaning of Jesus is defined by our experience, self-understanding, moral idealism, worldview, or philosophical system. The long history of Christology has been zigzagging between an ebionitic Jesus-ology and a docetic Logos-ology, and this kind of weaving from side to side abounds in contemporary christological treatises.

The Naming of Jesus

Each generation is addressed by the question Jesus put to his disciples on the road to Caesarea Philippi: "Who do people say that the Son of Man is?" They told him, "Some say John the Baptist, but others Elijah, and still others Jeremiah or one of the prophets." Then Jesus asked them, "But who do you say that I am?" Peter answered him, "You are the Messiah, the Son of the living God" (Matt 16:13-16). Ever since that time Christians have wondered about who Jesus really is and how best to name him. According to Mark's Gospel, such questions as these came pouring out in Jesus' own lifetime: Who is this one who teaches with authority? Who is this one who forgives sins? Who then is this one, that even the wind and the sea obey him? The essential task of preaching today is to answer this question: Who is this Jesus of Nazareth? What are we prepared to say about him and how to confess him? What is the meaning and relevance of Jesus in our global situation? Many people in our time would chime in with Saul of Tarsus on the road of Damascus, and cry out, "Who are you, Lord?" (Acts 9:5).

What do we have to go on in answering Jesus' original question, "But who do you say that I am?" We have the word and witness of those who loved him and knew him best, but we do not have as much as we would like to have. People are still eager to search in newly discovered ancient manuscripts for more information about Jesus of Nazareth. John came to the end of his Gospel and said, "But there are also many other things that Jesus did; if every one of them were written down, I suppose that the world itself could not contain the books that would be written" (21:25). Our libraries are now bulging with books that have been written imagining things that the authors wished Jesus had said or done, or worse, apologizing for some of the shocking things he did say and do. As Albert Schweitzer demonstrated in his classic study, *The Quest of the Historical Jesus,* "Each epoch found its reflection in Jesus; each individual created Him in accordance with his own character."[5]

No scholarly consensus yet exists regarding the true identity and meaning of Jesus of Nazareth. The infamous "Jesus Seminar" now under way has scholars voting on every saying in the four Gospels, but no overwhelming consensus is coming out of it. There may be something about both the sources and our methods that defies giving a definitive answer to Jesus' own question about his identity. There may also be something about the mystery of the person that accounts for the difficulty.

The history of Christology goes on, and today a new chapter is being written in the encounter with different claims to the way of salvation. Jaroslav Pelikan has recently written a wonderful book entitled *Jesus through the Centuries.*[6] We may believe with Hebrews (13:8) that "Jesus Christ is the same yesterday and today and forever," but our pictures and interpretations of Jesus change over the centuries and across the cultures. Pelikan's study of the history of portraying Jesus shows a remarkable variety of images. In the second century, Jesus was preached as the light of the Gentiles. To the Romans, Jesus was preached as the King of kings who gave people a choice between Christ and

Caesar, and many Christians lost their lives in the Roman Colosseum. In the third century, Jesus was proclaimed as the cosmic Logos, an apologetic bridge to the intelligentsia of the epoch, with highly ambiguous results. Adolf von Harnack referred to this period as the "Hellenization of Christianity." The Orthodox fathers, however, were careful to teach that the Logos was not essentially a metaphysical principle, although the word itself might suggest as much, but was nothing else than the flesh-and-blood person of Jesus Christ. To the Jews and the Greeks and the Romans, the early Christians confessed that their faith lies not in a set of laws, ideas, or beliefs, but in a person. Christianity is not an ism, like Platonism, Marxism, socialism, or capitalism. It is not essentially an abstract system of concepts and categories that can be detached from the person of the founder. In the Christian faith, the person of Jesus is the heart of the matter, the secret that makes it work.

Professor Pelikan takes us back through the centuries on a tour of all the major ways in which people have responded to the question, "But who do you say that I am?" Poets and monks and mystics and prophets and reformers have been grasped by this question. In Byzantine culture, Jesus is the perfect icon of God and the inspiration of all its mystical devotional literature. In medieval times, Jesus is depicted as a monk who transforms the world through monastic discipline and self-denial and embodies the ideals of poverty, chastity, and obedience. St. Francis of Assisi seemed to be such a convincing imitation of Christ that he earned an official designation by Pope Pius XI as "the second Christ." It is useful to follow Pelikan's presentation of the images of Jesus in all the centuries, but instead I need to hasten to the question of our own contemporary naming of Jesus.

The image of Jesus as liberator has captured the enthusiasm and commitment of more Christians around the world than perhaps any other. For many centuries the church of imperial Christendom pictured Jesus as the preserver of the status quo in state and church, as the chief guarantor of the eternal order of things reflected in temporal institutions. Today, at least in many parts of the world, people are looking to Jesus as the great source of the freedom for which they long, as the liberator who challenges every oppressive social or political or economic system. Every image applied to Jesus, however, involves a risk.

87

Who fills the image or symbol with its definitive meaning? Consider the Logos concept, for example. We can either approach Jesus with our minds made up about the meaning of Logos, taken from our favorite philosopher (for some it is Whitehead or Heidegger), or we can allow the history of Jesus as personal subject to define what we mean by the term. The paradigm instance of this kind of transformation of symbolic meaning occurred when the Jewish concept of the Messiah was radically transvaluated by Jesus' suffering and death on the cross. Jews were not looking for a crucified Messiah, but when they got him, the meaning of Messiahship was turned upside down.

We need to let the concrete history of Jesus as narrated and interpreted by the evangelists and apostles define for us the truest and deepest meaning of liberation. Some so-called liberation movements have little or nothing to do with the freedom that Jesus was sent on God's mission to deliver to all people. For many people liberation means license, licentiousness, libertinism, the freedom to be yourself, to do what you please, to secure your own. So that we are not guilty of promising people a liberation whose hidden agenda is the freedom of the autonomous self, the absolute narcissist who turns the whole world into a means of self-fulfillment and self-gratification, we need to let Jesus define for us the kind of liberation that God intends through his suffering, death, and resurrection. Jesus said, "My kingdom is not of this world," and so his liberation is not necessarily the kind the world is clamoring for.

To be sure, we would like to recruit Jesus for our own cause. We seem to have a powerful drive to define who Jesus is in accordance with our own needs and wishes. Instead of accommodating ourselves to Jesus' liberation movement, we find ourselves accommodating Jesus to ours. Books and articles have been written recently proving who Jesus is: Jesus is a guerrilla fighter; Jesus is a mushroom eater; Jesus is gay; Jesus is black; Jesus is a feminist (Christa). From the sublime to the ridiculous, Jesus is pictured as the perfect model of what each group understands itself to be. Like plastic surgeons making over the face of the patient in their own image, Jesus becomes a prisoner of our own fads and fashions.

No Other Name?

I know only one way to prevent us from veering to the side of an ebionitic Jesus or a docetic Christ: to conform our thinking to the normative words and witnesses to Jesus in the New Testament and the secondary derivative interpretations and definitions that we have in the Ecumenical Creeds of the ancient church. When we ignore or suspend these norms, Christology becomes so much clay that we model to make Jesus look like ourselves.

The question whether there is the promise of salvation in the name of Jesus, and in no other name, is fast becoming a life-and-death issue facing contemporary Christianity. In the churches this issue will become the test of fidelity to the gospel, a matter of *status confessionis* more urgent than any other. Legion are the Christologies now on the market that promise salvation through other names. As Langdon Gilkey puts it, religions are "roughly equal" in their ability to communicate saving grace and truth.

How can we know what is true salvation and true liberation? The people of God in the old covenant were convinced that only God can save. Israel was reminded time and time again that she could not save herself, nor could she be saved by the idols of the nations round about her. It is the Lord, and the Lord alone, who can save. Knowing full well that it was only God who could save, the first Christians nevertheless preached that Jesus was Savior and that there was salvation in no other name. Jesus saves his people from their sins (Matt 1:21); only in his name is there salvation (Acts 4:12); he is the pioneer of salvation (Heb 2:10). In these and many similar statements, Jesus is represented as doing what every good Jew knew only God could do. Sooner or later believers who wanted to think through their faith reasoned that if Jesus acts as God and if Jesus acts for God, as God's absolute plenipotentiary, then we have here in the person of Jesus the final revelation of God, Immanuel, God with us, God deep in the flesh and blood of this human being.

So also Jesus was declared to be the Lord, not merely in the everyday sense of sir or master, but in the Old Testament sense of the sacred name of God. Joel 2:32 states that "everyone who calls on the name of the Lord shall be saved," referring to Jahweh. When this passage is quoted in Acts 2:21, it is in the context of Peter's Pentecostal speech in which he declares that "God has made him [Jesus] both Lord and Messiah, this Jesus whom you crucified" (2:36). Many contemporaries became infuriated that Christians were so recklessly hijacking terms and titles reserved exclusively for the one God to speak of the identity of Jesus. To make matters worse, not only was Jesus addressed as Lord and Savior but he was also worshipped on the par with God the Father, Maker of heaven and earth. That is a scandal; that is an offense. It was so then; it is equally so today. To complete the story of this offense, I would have to go on to show how and why the early Christians modified the strict monotheism of their Hebrew origins into a christocentric trinitarian monotheism that finally reached its zenith in the Nicene-Constantinopolitan Creed.

According to the New Testament and the Nicene Creed, Jesus is the one and only Mediator between God and the world. First Tim 2:5 says: "For there is one God, and there is one mediator between God and humankind, Christ Jesus, himself human." Martin Luther would go on to rejoice in the "happy exchange" that occurred in Jesus Christ between God and humanity. Today Christians are challenged to make sense of their confession and experience of Jesus as Lord and Savior in the context of the missionary encounter of the world religions and modern ideologies. We must be ready to give good reasons for the hope that is in us and to witness credibly to our belief that Jesus means salvation and liberation, not for us alone who already believe but for the whole world and all those who do not yet believe in his name.

Because we are Christians interacting with people of other religions through evangelization, mission, dialogue, and service, the Spirit of God will open our lips both to new ways of proclaiming the gospel and to new ways of naming Jesus in light of the particular religious and cultural context to which we address the message of Christ. A myriad of contextualized forms contain one gospel, as the history of preaching and Christology shows. Many different earthen vessels contain one heavenly treasure, but this treasure is not separable from the personal identity and meaning of the Jesus of Nazareth recorded in the Scriptures. All the words and titles that New Testament Christianity used to preach Jesus as Savior had been used before in Jewish, Babylonian, Greek, and Roman religions. The gospel entered into a religiously pluralistic culture. Christianity did not invent a new language; it adopted fragments of the old languages and converted and baptized them in the process of preaching the eternal gospel of Jesus Christ. When Jesus is called the "Lamb of God," Jesus' own suffering and death on the cross invested that symbol with new meaning. The same is true about such words as Father, Son, Spirit, King, Lord, Messiah. All of these took on radically new meanings when their roots were planted in the soil of the gospel.

A similar adoptive conversion is happening around the world today. In the encounter of the gospel with the world religions, the new wine of the eternal gospel is being poured into the old skins of all the religious traditions of humanity, and the skins are bursting open. New history of mission and evangelization is being made. Many faithful witnesses have not surrendered the claim: No other name! No other gospel! Many others have, however; and their number seems to be growing, not only in academic circles but in church bureaucracies. The message we have to bring to the nations is still very much a matter in dispute. Christians are still martyred for their faith in parts of the world. Some offer gloomy predictions that Christianity is rapidly becoming a minority religion, and that worldly isms will sweep us off the face of the earth—secularism, atheism, Marxism, or some other. Billions of people do not know and believe in Jesus as the Christ of God. At the same time, millions are prepared to confess the name of Jesus no matter what it costs and to bear witness that God is in Christ working out the world's salvation.

Those who stand in the Reformation tradition of Martin Luther place a strong emphasis on the sole mediatorship of Jesus Christ. The righteousness of God and the justification of the sinful world have been communicated to the world on account of Christ alone, because in Christ God has broken down the barriers of human sinfulness and God's wrath. The overwhelming power of God's love drives Christians to meet all other neighbors in the sure confidence that this love is wide enough to include all who are now separated from their maker, that Christ died for all and was raised for the world's justification. Many ways of salvation are not needed, because the one way God has revealed in Jesus Christ is sufficient for all.

A Theology of the Religions

Recently Christian theology and the scientific study of the religions have met like long lost relatives on the common ground

91

of the world religions. At the beginning, the meeting is somewhat awkward, because the relatives do not know just what to say to each other. They have learned to speak such different languages, and they function in such different contexts. Some have spent the major part of their lives trying to understand one religion faithfully, and they do this as a matter of personal conviction. Others have crossed over to study another religion or two and have learned to enter into them by using scholarly methods of inquiry, but they do so more as a matter of academic vocation than as an existential commitment.

The watershed date is the end of World War II. Just prior to World War II, Hendrik Kraemer had published *The Christian Message in a Non-Christian World* in preparation for the 1938 World Missionary Conference, which was meeting in Tambaran, India. This scarce book bore the spirit of radical discontinuity that Karl Barth had first enunciated in his commentary on Romans. Barth's negative judgment on religion gave no compelling reason to wrestle theologically with the religions. The early Barth said that all religion was sacrificed on Golgotha. The religious gods died on Good Friday. Religion is the affair of the godless person. Religion is a vain human attempt at self-salvation. After World War II, however, the climate began to change in favor of a more positive evaluation of religion and the religions that inspired new attempts to forge some links between Christian theology and the scientific study of the religions. New hypotheses concerning the relationship between Christianity and the other major world religions have been conceived, older ones have been revised, but none has gained a monopoly. The World Council of Churches has been promoting interreligious dialogue, but it operates with no coherent Christian theology of the religions. Recently the Lutheran World Federation has also begun to explore relations with religions other than Christian; and as is customary among Lutherans, its first efforts have focused on theological issues that inquire specifically into the resources of the Lutheran theological heritage that bear on this interreligious topic.[7]

The phrase *a theology of the religions* is quite new. In the university catalogues of divinity schools and schools of religion, we find courses with such titles as philosophy of religion, psychology of religion, phenomenology of religion, the history of religions, but only very rarely do we find this newcomer, a theology of the religions, or some variant of it. A Christian theology of the religions is the name given to that discipline which aims to think about the world religions in light of the Christian faith.[8] Heretofore, the religions were relegated to a marginal place in the scheme of Christian dogmatics, somewhere near the end as a kind of missiological postscript.

A Christian theology of the religions calls upon theology to go beyond merely reflecting on the symbols and stories of the Christian tradition. Not only Christianity but also other religions become the object of critical theological inquiry. Most theologians are not yet accustomed to this new challenge. Since the Enlightenment, however, Christian theology has met one challenge after the other. The challenge of history to think about Christian origins in a fully critical manner came first. Then came the challenge of critical epistemology, with its turn to the subject, followed by the challenge of science, with its evolutionary hypothesis. Today the challenge is the plurality of religions.

Religious pluralism is not new. Christianity was born in the maelstrom of a variety of Jewish, Greek, Roman, and Oriental religious and philosophical currents. From the beginning, the tiny Christian movement had to struggle to establish its own identity and viability in the ancient world. Christianity was attacked by the Jews as a heresy, persecuted by the Romans as a seditious movement, ridiculed as a contemptible myth by the Hellenistic philosophers, and threatened by the popular cults and mystery religions. Within three centuries, the status of Christianity changed from being an illegal and ridiculous sect to being the official religion of the Roman Empire. Then religious pluralism became drastically diminished during the age of Christendom. New today is the increasing awareness that Christianity is just one among many religions in the global community. Religions are no longer confined to particular boundaries. The flow and speed of interreligious traffic have increased tremendously, and a wealth of knowledge about other religions has been accumulated over the past two centuries. Christianity is now confronted by a counter-missionary thrust on the part of some other religions like Islam, Hinduism, and Buddhism.

The old ways of pigeonholing the religions do not seem to work anymore. Sometimes the religions were judged to be preparations for the gospel; sometimes, the wiles and ways of the devil; sometimes, alternative intimations of the one true God. These dogmatic judgments have been challenged by the sheer gravity of the empirical and historical data analyzed in terms of their own cultural and linguistic contexts. But no new prevailing systematic theological paradigm has replaced the older constructions. We face not only a plurality of religions but also a plurality of theologies. In addition, we are mired in a relativism that claims that all the religions are equally endowed with powers of liberation and salvation. The dominant feeling today seems to be that basically all religions say the same thing and lead to the same end, only they do so in terms of different ritual symbols and language systems. When Christian theologians take this view, it may occur to some Buddhist to congratulate them on becoming "anonymous Buddhists."

In the face of religious relativism, Christian theology will look around for some way to secure the exclusive claim of the gospel to universal validity. The basic question is how to conceive of the act of God in Jesus Christ as having ultimate significance for all people at all times in every place. Christian theologians have learned from experience the difficulty of trying to make good this exclusive claim (no matter how broadly they project the inclusivity of its content) without being accused of being so dogmatically prejudiced as to be unfit for interreligious dialogue. At this point methodological rigor is called for. Prejudice has now often shifted to the side of those who claim scientific objectivity in dealing with religion and the religions. That all scholars of religion acknowledge the presuppositions with which they operate is a matter of methodological fairness. There is no presuppositionless approach to any of the great human passions of sex, politics, and religion, nor to any of the loftier visions of truth, beauty, and goodness. A Christian theology of the religions calls for a candid approach that should acknowledge its presuppositions clearly rather than obscurely. Why should anyone want a Christian theology of the world religions that plays by the old rules? For one thing, new rules might expose as a sham the make-believe objectivity of some practitioners of the various sciences of religion.

Christian theology bears a particular burden. Its presuppositions are burning convictions that are hard to hide. The

Christian thinker is a whole person whose captivity to the gospel is freely and joyously articulated in every dimension of life. The Christian scholar is a slave of Jesus Christ, in whom God is truly disclosed, full of grace and truth. There is no way to bracket out this commitment when dealing with religious and ethical matters. Scholars with presuppositions less clear and distinct may see the speck in a Christian theology of the religions but fail to see the log in their own approaches. Scholars cannot measure things without some kind of ruler. For Christians, the ruler is Jesus Christ and no other. Jesus Christ cannot be subsumed under some other category that is presumably more adequate to interpret the religions of the world.

Logos Spermatikos or *Logos Ensarkos?*

The exclusive claim of the gospel continues to be a thorn in the flesh of those who would postulate the equality of the religions. The current pluralistic theory of religions, which enjoys a high popularity in some academic circles, advocates that the incarnational dogma and its exclusive claim be deconstructed to myth, fiction, pretense, illusion, opium, crutch, escape, or all of the above. I do not intend to address the deconstruction approach in this chapter. I have already argued at some length that it cuts the Gordian knot. Christian theology cannot relinquish the claim of eschatological finality in connection with the historical figure of Jesus without surrendering the ground principle of Christian identity.

Two other approaches, however, have shared a long history of controversy. One is along the line of the ancient patristic doctrine of the Logos, which we have argued moves in a docetic direction. This approach leads to a large Christ-principle universally present and operative in the various religions, philosophies, and ideologies apart from the gospel proclamation about Jesus and the kingdom. Justin Martyr used the Stoic concept of the seminal Logos (*Logos spermatikos*) to account for all the truth, beauty, and goodness to be found outside of Christianity. The pagans received all these splendid things through the Logos whose seeds have been spread throughout the world. This theory found classical expression in the natural theology of the scholastics and in the rational religion of the Enlightenment. It achieved contemporary expression in Tillich's notion of the "latent church" and in Rahner's concept of "Anonymous Christianity." The theory, in whatever particular rendition, is attractive for a number of reasons. It permits a generous estimate of what God is doing beyond the walls of the church, and it offers a point of contact between biblical religion and the virtues and values of other religions. Specifically, the missionary task of the church can use it as a bridge for its own work of translating the gospel into the language of other cultures. The theologians of younger churches are also attracted to this doctrine today because it offers a basis for a positive attitude toward the spiritual heritage of their ancestors and non-Christian neighbors.

The second approach in the Christian tradition is slender and intermittent. It does not enjoy classical status, and it is most clearly represented by Luther. It constitutes a break with the Logos outside the flesh, the *Logos asarkos* of the patristic-medieval synthesis. For Luther, the *Logos spermatikos* and the cross of Christ don't get along well together. One is philosophical speculation; the other is the Word of God in the flesh, the *Logos ensarkos*. The Logos is a universal principle; Jesus is a concrete person; Jesus is the enfleshed Logos. The subject is Jesus, who gives to the predicate, Logos, its definitive content and meaning. The Logos idea of John is transformed by being filled with the story of Jesus' life, death, and resurrection. This incarnational current is nonreversible, which the Lutherans later maintained against the Calvinists in the Lord's Supper controversy. The Logos is never without the flesh (*numquam extra carnem*).

The crucial significance of Christ is maintained in either of the two rival interpretations. For the one, the Christ is an ideal principle of religion and morality universally manifest and is, therefore, certainly also present in Jesus to the degree of eminence directly proportionate to the intensity of one's personal piety. Pietists like Schleiermacher will elevate Jesus' status to the highest possible potency; yet, in this pietistic approach Jesus is different from the rest of humanity only by degree. For the other interpretation, Christ is a person of history in whom God is present in the moil and toil of Jesus' life and death. In one view the linkage between the Logos and Jesus is very loose; in the other it is very tight.

Some theologians are sympathetic with the intentions of the ancient Logos Christology, but they do not believe that it can bear the heavy traffic that flows between the religions in their concrete histories. Ernst Benz, one of the pioneers in promoting a theology linked to the history of religions, said that despite its good intentions "the traditional Logos theology and its modern versions proves itself to be a theological ell which is too short to measure our modern consciousness of history."[9] There are other objections as well. In the age of Christendom, the Logos doctrine became the substitute for the expectation of the coming Messiah, and contributed to the de-eschatologization of Christian faith. With the loss of eschatological hope, the engine that propelled the global mission of the church began to idle. Another objection, one raised even by Paul Knitter and John Hick, is that Logos Christology amounts to a pseudo-Christocentrism that aims to uphold the centrality of Christ in a way that is artificial, as artificial as upholding the old Ptolemaic view of the universe by adding a few epicycles to deal with the new scientific discoveries of astronomy.

The classical way of constructing the relationship between special revelation in the gospel and general revelation in other religions hinged on the distinction between the concrete Logos in the flesh (*ensarkos*) and the universal Logos outside the flesh (*asarkos*). Only in modern theology has the *Logos spermatikos* been granted a soteriological function that renders the incarnation unnecessary. In traditional Lutheran terminology, this means that a number of distinctions have collapsed, such as the distinction between God hidden and revealed, between law and gospel, between the two kingdoms, and so forth. Some Catholic and Protestant theologians speak of the religions as "ways of salvation," and this puts even more distinctions at risk as we try to develop a theological theory of the relation of Christianity to other religions.

Phenomenologically, all religions are by definition ways of salvation. The proper business of religion is to save, but not all salvation is the same. A person who seeks salvation in mind-altering drugs gets a different salvation than a person who seeks salvation in transcendental meditation. No generic salvation exists, no salvation to which the various religions can merely provide different labels. Those who have converted from one religion to another are the first to provide the conclusive testimonies. The history of religions provides us with different

models of salvation and different ways that the models are sup-
posed to work. When the slaves in Egypt cried out for salvation,
to be released from their oppression, Moses led the exodus out
of Egypt. Similarly, if salvation is the experience of illumination,
those who follow the way of the Buddha find it. Each religion
advertises the particular salvation it promises those who are
willing to follow its way.

The dialogue between the religions leads finally to a dis-
closure of the sacred and saving mystery that lies within the
horizon of each religious tradition. Participants in dialogue meet
and challenge each other by witnessing to the deepest mystery
of life that defines their being and future. I do not think it should
be so readily assumed that some current variant of the Logos
principle is the most useful presupposition of interreligious dialogue. This concept of the larger Christ manifest in all the
religions is a way of co-opting them. It makes them appear to
be mere echoes of what we know already or seeds of the same
stalk that grows in our garden.

Jesus and the World Religions

Christians today are challenged to make sense of their confession
of Jesus as God and Savior in the context of the world religions.
Our Christian confession of the identity and meaning of Jesus
meets a world in which the name of Jesus has already spread to
all corners of the world. We are asked by Scripture to give a
reason for the hope that is in us. We are asked to answer not
only Jesus' question, "But who do you say that I am?" but also
the question of our contemporaries: Why do you confess Jesus
to be the Lord and Liberator of life, to be the Son of God and
the Savior of humanity? What is the meaning of these exalted
titles bestowed on Jesus of Nazareth, whose life and ministry
were terminated by death on the cross? In the coming dialogue
of the great religions, men and women of faith have a desire to
learn from one another the central affirmations of their different
faiths. We must be prepared to witness credibly to our belief
that Jesus means God's presence for us, and not for us alone,
but for the whole world that God so loved that people might
receive the gift of salvation in his name.

Most of the religions can quite readily revere Jesus as a
teacher or prophet, as a spiritual leader or moral example. Jews

and Muslims and Hindus and Buddhists can accept Jesus as one of the prophets, revelations, avatars, or Bodhisattvas. Each of these religions has reserved a special place for Jesus in its hierarchy of sacred names and symbols. When Christians meet their neighbors of other persuasions, their dialogue can proceed on many levels. They share many interests bearing on world peace, human rights, cultural enrichment, religious tolerance, and care for the earth. These are all very important issues, but then there is that other special dimension of faith dealing with the deepest mystery of the world and the meaning of life.

We cannot expect that people of other faiths have the same interest in Jesus and experience of salvation that Christians have had in the last two thousand years. Christians should meet others at their own level of experience and knowledge and pick up the conversation at that point. The God revealed in Jesus Christ is the same God hiddenly at work throughout the world in all the religions of humankind. God has not left himself without a witness anywhere in the world, and the Jesus they have heard about is the same Jesus in whose name we have received grace and truth. Our dialogue, therefore, is not one-sided, with everything coming from us and our getting nothing back in return.

CHRISTIANS AND JEWS

In the dialogue between Christians and Jews today, we have come to a new appreciation of the Jewishness of Jesus. While this dialogue is helping Gentile Christians to recover their Hebrew roots, Jewish scholars are displaying a new openness to Jesus as their brother. Jesus of Nazareth is the link between Jews and Christians. Jews come from the same household of faith and are blood brothers and sisters of Jesus. Some of us Gentiles have been adopted into the family of God through our faith in Jesus as the Messiah of Israel, and thus both Jews and Christian Gentiles are sons and daughters of the history of faith beginning with Abraham and Sarah. In our dialogue with Jews, we are reminded that Judaism and Christianity are both messianic religions. Jesus is the bond of union between all Jews and Gentiles who confess faith in Jahweh whom Jesus addressed as "Abba." Yet, there is a separation between Jews and Christians, and Jesus is the real difference.

99

For Christians, Jesus is the Messiah; but Jews are still waiting for the coming of the Messiah and the dawn of the new
age. From a Jewish point of view, nothing is final and exclusive
about Jesus of Nazareth. Jews will continue to pray for the
coming of the Messiah; Christians will continue to pray to the
Messiah who has already come. This Messianic reference, therefore, unites Jews and Christians but is the decisive difference
between the blood brothers and sisters of Jesus and all his gentile
friends and followers. The separation between Jews and Christians is only temporary. Paul says in Romans that in the end all
the Jews will acknowledge Jesus as the Messiah of Israel, which
is an eschatological conviction contrary to present trends.

ISLAM

Unlike the literature of Judaism, Islam's sacred book, the
Qu'ran, contains explicit teaching about Jesus. Muslims are not
opposed to Jesus. The Qu'ran speaks of Jesus in a favorable
light. For Muslims, Jesus is a prophet and messenger of Allah,
even a suffering servant of God. The Qu'ran declares Jesus the
Word and Truth of God, in a special lineage of messengers along
with Moses, David, and the prophet Muhammad. Here we have
a point of contact for dialogue with Muslims about the relation
between God and the messenger of God.

For Christians, the union between God and Jesus is the root
of the doctrine of the Trinity. For Muslims, such a personal
union drives Christians into what looks like tritheism, the belief
in three Gods. The Qu'ran says: "They are unbelievers who say
that God is threefold. No god there is but one God" (Sura 5,
78). For Christians, too, Jesus is a prophet; but he is more than
a prophet because he assumed God's authority, forgave sins, and
fulfilled the law and the prophets. On the other hand, the Qu'ran
even speaks of the resurrection of Jesus from the dead, and there
is also a reference to Jesus' ascension into heaven. In some sense,
Muslims affirm that Jesus is alive, that he was taken up body,
soul, and spirit into the life and glory of God in heaven.

HINDUISM

When Christians go to the Far East, they find that the image
of Jesus has already made an impact on modern Hinduism.

Gandhi was inspired by the message and example of Jesus. He said, "It is this Sermon [on the Mount] that endeared Jesus to me." He also said, "Although I cannot claim to be a Christian in a confessional sense, still the example of Jesus' suffering is a factor in the make-up of my fundamental belief in non-violence that guides all my worldly and temporary actions."[10] The Christian theologian M. M. Thomas, of Bangalore, India, has said that the image of the historical Jesus must be the starting point of the Christian dialogue with people in India, because it contains the power to motivate people to meet the needs of the poor and the oppressed.

No one has any illusions that it is easy to confess Christ today in India. One problem is the severe political restrictions imposed on evangelization and conversions from Hinduism to Christianity; another problem is that traditional Hinduism can incorporate the figure of the Christ into the pantheon along with Krishna, Rama, Isvara, Purusha, and other divinities. Its tolerance is limited by the demand that Christians give up the exclusive claim of the gospel and of Jesus being the one and only Lord and Savior of the world. Jesus may be accepted as a yogi or guru, as one among any, or he may be accepted as one of many avataras, one of the many incarnations of the transcendent divine Reality. We do know, however, that the dialogue with neo-Hinduism has reached our own shores because we see the young Hindu missionaries selling the Upanishads or the Bhagavadgita at our major airports.

BUDDHISM

The most advanced dialogue is between Christians and Buddhists. Many Christian theologians have found among Buddhists a sophisticated openness ready for a mutual conversation concerning the things of the spirit. Buddhists interpret Jesus and his message in light of their own understanding of the Buddha and his teachings. Comparisons and differences can readily be drawn between Christ and Buddha. Just as Jesus is the Christ, the anointed One, so also Gautama is the Buddha, the enlightened One. The truth of Buddha's teaching on enlightenment, however, does not depend on its relationship to the historical Gautama in the same way as the Christian message

101

of salvation depends on its connection with the historical person of Jesus. Nevertheless, there are striking comparisons between the story of Gautama and the story of Jesus. Both of them became poor wandering preachers with a message of salvation. Both of them gathered disciples and taught them in the everyday language of the people by using stories, parables, and proverbs. Both of them criticized and conflicted with the religious authorities, the scribes, and the priests of their respective religious traditions. Both of them demanded of people a change of heart and direction, total commitment, and no halfway measures. Both of them saw that people are afflicted by a tendency to care too much for the things of this passing world and to render things absolute that are purely relative. Both of them saw an inordinate drive in human beings to put themselves first, call it selfishness, greed, egoism, or whatever.

What a sharp contrast, however, between the twisted figure of Jesus hanging on a cross, the price he paid for bringing in the kingdom of God's love, and the smiling Buddha sitting on a lotus blossom, exuding tranquility, harmony, and good humor! The crucified Christ experienced rejection, failure, agony, and dereliction as a result of the supreme sacrifice of love poured out for the world. Here again the cross is the criterion of the chief point of difference between the gospel of Christ and all other systems of salvation. Paul called the cross foolishness to the Gentiles and a stone of stumbling to the Jews.

[6]

The Trinity Is the Model of the Church's Unity and Mission

AT OXFORD UNIVERSITY is a gigantic painting of a man and a small boy by the sea. The painting is based on a story told about the great St. Augustine, bishop of Hippo, who was writing his famous book on the Trinity, the greatest classic ever written on the subject. As the story goes, Augustine was walking along the coast one day when he met a small boy pouring sea water into a hole in the ground. Augustine watched him for some time and eventually asked him what he was doing. "I'm pouring the Mediterranean Sea into this hole," replied the boy. "Don't be so stupid," admonished Augustine, "you can't fit the sea into that little hole. You're wasting your time." "And so are you," the boy shot back, "trying to write a book on God."

I have always wanted to write a book about the Trinity, but the often repeated refrain that the Trinity is an incomprehensible mystery has made me feel too stupid to try. How can we pour the mystery of the Trinity into the small hole occupied by the finite human mind? How can we think and speak and write about God whom the great tradition has defined as essentially inconceivable, ineffable, and inexpressible? More and more I have come to realize that the spirit of Plato lies behind this intimidation. The spirit of Plato came to permeate the mainstream of Christian theology rather than the Spirit of Jesus, the Jesus who invites us to know the essential being of God based on his coming under the conditions of our human experience and knowledge.

My thesis is that the current renewal of trinitarian theology provides us with an inexhaustible resource for bringing new initiatives and insights to the ecumenical quest for Christian unity and the worldwide mission of the church. This new thinking on the Trinity began with the two greatest theologians of the twentieth century, Karl Barth and Karl Rahner, a Protestant and a Roman Catholic. At no point in contemporary theology do we find such transconfessional unity as in the new construction of the doctrine of the Trinity. Protestants and Catholics are drawing freely from both of the Karls; and all of these are making connections with the Greek Fathers, especially the Cappadocians, whose voice lives in the theology of Eastern Orthodoxy. Within this trinitarian theology, we find our deepest roots in the common ground of the one faith that all our traditions claim to confess; and that one faith, above everything else, is the essential condition of the communion of all churches and their common witness to the gospel.

The number of theologians who form a kind of trinitarian school of thought is not large. The most notable among them are Eberhard Jüngel, Wolfhart Pannenberg, Jürgen Moltmann, Walter Kasper, Leonardo Boff, and Robert Jenson. Each of them is making major contributions to a profound reappropriation of the specifically Christian doctrine of the Triune God.[1] Although there certainly are differences among them, they converge in their acceptance of Karl Rahner's now famous thesis: "The 'economic' Trinity is the 'immanent' Trinity and the 'immanent' Trinity is the 'economic' Trinity."[2] Their disagreements arise chiefly from the way in which they draw out the implications of this thesis for understanding the reciprocal relations among the three persons of the Trinity and through their understanding of the little word "is" that connects the "immanent" and the "economic" aspects of the Trinity. For the benefit of anyone who has forgotten what this distinction classically means, "immanent" refers to God's eternal being in and for himself and "economic" refers to God's incarnational presence in history "for us and for our salvation." How are the eternal and historical poles of God's being and activity related? Because the immanent and the economic Trinity are so closely connected, perhaps even identical, the Trinity must be a source and model for our thinking about the church, its unity, and its mission.

The unity and mission of the church coincide directly with the salvation-historical workings of the Son and of the Spirit. To know the history of God's trinitarian activity in the messianic ministry of Jesus and the apostolic mission of the Spirit is to know the starting point and purpose of the church. The church participates, as a whole and in all its parts, in the movements of the divine sending of the Son into the world and of the Spirit into the church. It participates in these movements so that it may become a sign and instrument of God's eschatological re-possession of the world and so that, by means of its fulfillment, it may irradiate the glory of God.

Renewing Trinitarian Theology

Karl Rahner formulated his trinitarian axiom in order to overcome the doctrine's dysfunctional place in theology and the Christian life. He lamented that "Christians are, in their practical life, almost mere 'monotheists.' We must be willing to admit that, should the doctrine of the Trinity have to be dropped as false, the major part of religious literature could well remain virtually unchanged."[3] The nonfunctionality of the Trinity in the Christian life is linked to the fact that, as Rahner says, "the Trinity occupies a rather isolated position in the total dogmatic system. To put it crassly . . . when the treatise is concluded, its subject is never brought up again. . . . It is as though this mystery has been revealed for its own sake, and that even after it has been made known to us, it remains, *as a reality,* locked up within itself. We make statements about it, but as a reality it has nothing to do with us at all."[4]

Rahner claims that the consignment of the Trinity to theological and spiritual irrelevance can be traced to Thomas Aquinas, who for the first time divided the discussion of God into two sharply separated treatises: "On the One God" (*De Deo Uno*), concerned with natural theology; and "On the Triune God" (*De Deo Trino*), concerned with revelation. Thus, Rahner said, "the treatise of the Trinity locks itself in even more splendid isolation, with the ensuing danger that the religious mind finds it devoid of interest. It looks as if everything which matters for us in God has already been said in the treatise *On the One God.*"[5]

Karl Rahner wrote those words in the 1960s as part of the effort to renew Catholic dogmatics by constructing it on the foundations of the biblical history of salvation.[6] Three decades before, Karl Barth had already stipulated that "the reality of God which meets us in revelation is His reality in all the depths of eternity."[7] No different reality of God is behind his revelation—as though the true essence of God inheres in his oneness, with his threefoldness lying at a lower level of metaphorical language. Only by overcoming the separation between the oneness and the threeness is it possible to connect the mystery of the Trinity with the nature of the church and its mission.

Barth, Rahner, and the current trinitarian theologians are thus going against the stream of the Western pattern of dealing with the Trinity. In modern Protestant theology, the doctrine of the Trinity does not only languish in "splendid isolation"[8] from the primary discussion of God in the dogmatic prolegomena but, in many places, is discarded altogether. Immanuel Kant exercised an enormous influence on the school of Albrecht Ritschl, which included such famous names as Adolf von Harnack and Wilhelm Herrmann. Kant decreed: "From the doctrine of the Trinity, taken literally, nothing whatsoever can be gained for practical purposes, even if one believed that one comprehended it—and less still if one is conscious that it surpasses all our concepts."[9] Friedrich Schleiermacher had no taste for the Trinity and regarded the doctrine as "not an immediate utterance concerning the Christian self-consciousness, but only a combination of such utterances."[10] He dealt with the Trinity only in the Conclusion of his dogmatics, which only encouraged his followers to regard it as a highly problematic theologoumenon. Cyril Richardson concluded that the doctrine of the Trinity is loaded with confusions because from the start it was an "artificial construct."[11] In the nineteenth century, the disciples of Hegel and Schelling kept trinitarian thinking alive. With them, however, it often veered away from the Christian faith and life into abstract metaphysical speculations, which only reinforced the suspicion that the Trinity did not grow out of the soil of the gospel but was a dispensable product of what Harnack called the "Hellenization of Christianity." By the time the Protestant tradition reached Karl Barth, the doctrine of the Trinity was all but dead.

Repeating an Old Error

Barth's rediscovery of the biblical roots of the Trinity and its flowering in Patristic theology did not make its mark only in the academic world. It bore fruit from the beginning in the conciliar documents of the World Council of Churches, those that dealt with both ecumenical and missiological issues. Tracing the theology of the Trinity within the history of the modern ecumenical movement became a worthwhile task in itself and resulted in the present study document of the Commission on Faith and Order, entitled "Confessing One Faith, Towards an Ecumenical Explication of the Apostolic Faith as Expressed in the Nicene-Constantinopolitan Creed." The strong trinitarian emphasis of this document bodes well for the future, but it has not come about by accident. At Bangalore, Wolfhart Pannenberg called for Faith and Order to take up this project of explaining the apostolic faith on the basis that the Nicene-Constantino-politan Creed of 381 was a means of calling "the churches to the goal of visible unity *in one faith* and in one eucharistic fellowship."[12] At Bangalore, the Commission on Faith and Order was challenged to take up the ideological agendas of some pressure groups that would, in effect, threaten to derail the ecumenical quest for unity that had been based on faith rather than politics. The consultants on the apostolic-faith project included a number of Orthodox theologians—such as Nicolas Lossky, Vitaly Borovoy, Thomas Hopko, and John Zizioulas—whose faith is without doubt centered in the confession of the Triune God revealed in Jesus Christ, centered to a degree that has never been the case in Western Catholicism and Protestant Christianity. Just as the "Baptism, Eucharist, and Ministry" document of Faith and Order has been extremely effective in engendering theological conversations within and between churches on basic issues that both unite and divide, so might we expect this study of the apostolic faith to call churches to a broad perspective on the salvific work of the Triune God in creation, reconciliation, and fulfillment.

Such a trinitarian perspective will be perhaps even more crucial in ordering the thinking of the churches concerning their mission together. As early as 1963, Lesslie Newbigin invited "the missionary movement to bind to itself afresh the strong Name of the Trinity."[13] What was he worried about? He asked, "Why is there not more vigour in the missionary work of the Churches which share in the ecumenical movement?" Is it not because there is "a deep uncertainty in the Churches concerning the uniqueness and finality of the Gospel itself?"[14] The church will not be able to discern the missionary significance of God's revelation in Jesus Christ "except within the framework of a fully and explicitly trinitarian doctrine of God."[15] Newbigin acknowledged that his little book on the Trinity, *Trinitarian Faith and Today's Mission,* would lack the "depth and solidity" to accomplish what is needed for the ecumenical and missionary movements.[16] Twenty-five years later, Bishop Newbigin has expressed alarm that the trinitarian and christological foundations of the universal mission of the gospel are crumbling in the newer pluralistic theologies of religion.[17] These pluralistic theologies relativize the universal validity of the gospel of Jesus Christ. They represent a radical shift in belief and a fundamental deconstruction of the trinitarian paradigm within which Jesus Christ, in his uniqueness and universality, has defined the nature and aim of the gospel's cross-cultural mission to the nations. The consequences of this shift of paradigm are far-reaching. The missionary experience of the churches in the nineteenth century gave birth to the ecumenical movement. If the missionary movement now loses its flaming center in the gospel of Jesus Christ as structured by God's trinitarian dealings with the world, the whole ecumenical movement is bound to falter. It will lose its raison d'être because the entire ecumenical journey toward the reunification of the churches has been motivated by the missionary vision of Jesus' prayer to his Father in the upper room the night before he died: "I ask . . . that they may be one . . . so that the world may know that you have sent me" (John 17:20-21).

Bishop Newbigin senses the threat coming from the new pluralistic theology of the religions that dominates the academic centers engaged in the scientific study of the religions. Such dominance would be nothing to worry about except that the current ideologies underlying the pluralistic model for dialogue with the world religions are based in the relativistic ecumenism of the World Council of Churches and its denominational satellites. Paul Knitter, who is an advocate of the new relativistic theory of the religions, has warned: "There are Christian theologians who, in their efforts to understand and dialogue with other religions, are clearly and seriously questioning the finality or definitive normativity of Christ and Christianity. They are still a minority voice within the Christian churches. Yet their voice is growing stronger. A new consciousness within Christianity seems to be forming."[18] There is no question that Paul Knitter is right, and that is exactly what Bishop Newbigin is worried about. If this theology is still a minority within the Christian churches, however, it has won hands down within the religious studies' departments of universities and divinity schools. It is also rapidly making inroads into the liberal and mainstream denominational seminaries, which are always prone to assimilate the theology of nonconfessional centers for the academic study of religion.

Paul Knitter is an astute observer of developments in twentieth-century theology. He observes that there has been an evolution taking place "within Christian consciousness from the early part of this century, an evolution from ecclesiocentrism to christocentrism to theocentrism."[19] All of which he applauds; but what kind of theocentrism does he have in mind? It is a nontrinitarian monotheistic theocentrism. The pluralistic religious paradigm opts for a theocentricity at the expense of the christological origin of the doctrine of the Trinity. For believers in Christ, however, the trinitarian confession is the Christian way to speak of God. In the new theocentric model of religious pluralism, the Christology becomes so reductionistically negligible that only the lowest possible christological ideas are considered worthy of modern belief. The antichristocentric theocentrists are prepared to speak of some other God than the One who identifies himself with Jesus of Nazareth. They trumpet forth the virtues of that "mere monotheism" of which Rahner wrote. By unravelling the doctrine of the Trinity, they surrender the Christology from which it evolved. The doctrine of the Trinity has its base of origin in Christology and nothing else! Only Christology makes the confession of the triune God imperative. The doctrine of the Trinity is the theological framework for Christology and ecclesiology, for the event of salvation and the gospel mission.

If the new pluralistic theology of the religions gains ascendancy, the death of both the ecumenical and the missionary movements will ensue. This new theology is really a relapse into the nineteenth-century monotheism that tried to think about God apart from Jesus and, consequently, to think of Jesus as though he were only one in a series of prophets. The academic establishment in America produces many books about God that do not even broach the doctrine of the Trinity because they do not start from the salvation-historical Christology on which the doctrine rests—books by David Tracy, Langdon Gilkey, Gordon Kaufmann, Schubert Ogden, John Cobb, Tom Driver, Sallie McFague, James Gustafson, Paul Knitter, John Hick, and Mark C. Taylor, just to name a few. Virtually all schools of theology in America (process, liberationist, feminist, pragmatist, deconstructionist, postmodern, or whatever) repeat the fallacy that Karl Rahner traces back to Thomas Aquinas—separating the two treatises on the one God and on the triune God—except that the American theologians seldom get around to the Trinity.

In American theology, the doctrine of the Trinity has disintegrated into what Rahner dubbed "mere monotheism." To be sure, this follows the Western tradition that begins with a general discussion about the existence and essence of the one God. Nothing would prevent American theology from then proceeding to a discussion of the trinity of persons if it had not surrendered the biblical, ecclesial, and christological reasons for doing so. Knitter boasts that twentieth-century theology has been moving away from ecclesiocentrism and Christocentrism to theocentrism and, thereby, above and beyond the God of the gospel narrative concerning the relations of the Father, the Son, and the Spirit. We are confronting head-on the christological issue. Any move away from Christology as the Christian way of speaking and thinking about God leads automatically to something other than the trinitarian pattern of God-talk. What results is some kind of unitarian theocentrism that invites us to think of God without Christ and vice versa.

The spirit of the old liberalism of Adolf von Harnack is behind the whole project, as exemplified in his statement: "The Gospel, as Jesus proclaimed it, has to do with the Father only and not with the Son."[20] The pluralistic model of theology teaches that all the religions are roughly equal as ways of salvation and that Christ is only one of many paths that lead to God. That Christ is unique, central, definitive, and normative for the Christian understanding of revelation and salvation is a conviction that is equated with the cultural parochialism of the primitive mind and considered to be an aspect of the old myth of God incarnate, which is not intelligible or credible to the modern mind. Gone is the motive for mission! Jesus Christ is not the Way and the Truth and the Life for all! I agree with the verdict of Hans Küng:

> What is proclaimed today as "brand-new" teaching often proves to be the old teaching from the liberal Protestant stable. Such people do indeed hear God speaking through Jesus "as well" but have abandoned his normativity and "finality" (conclusiveness). They have put him on the level of other prophets alongside others (Christ together with other religions or other revealers, saviours, Christs) and so have lost all criteria for the discernment of spirits. Against such liberalism the protest of Karl Barth and "dialectical theology" . . . was a necessary corrective. To go back in this direction is no progress.[21]

Drawing on the Biblical Witness

We are faced fundamentally with two types of theology in contemporary Christianity. The one anchors itself in the biblical witness to God's salvation-historical dealings with the world, centered in the revelation of Christ and elaborated in the doctrine of the Trinity as a tripersonal communion of reciprocal relations. I argue that this vision of God has positive implications for the ecumenical and missionary future of the churches. The other type bases itself not on the biblical witness but on an alleged shift in contemporary Christian consciousness, which its advocates call a "Copernican revolution" or a "paradigm-shift."[22] This view calls for a so-called wider ecumenism that integrates all the religions into a pluralistic theocentric model, none occupying the center, none claiming a truth that is the criterion of all others. God and not Jesus Christ is placed at the center of the universe of faiths. This approach claims to hold great promise for the future of interreligious dialogue, but it surely cuts the heart out of the church's evangelistic mission. The implications are equally disastrous for the quest for unity because, by relativizing the common christological center of the churches, it allows each one to assert its own particularity as center, which brings about a complete reversal of direction in the ecumenical movement.

I turn now to the way in which the new trinitarian model for theology is constructed so that I can draw out some of its positive implications for ecumenism and missiology. Moltmann makes a statement that virtually characterizes all the new trinitarians: "If the biblical testimony is chosen as point of departure, then we shall have to start from the three Persons of the history of Christ. If philosophical logic is made the starting point, then the enquirer proceeds from the One God."[23] The new trinitarians do not believe that their inquiry need start with a philosophical principle of absolute unity before trying to understand the biblical history of the relations between three personal identities—the Father, Jesus of Nazareth, and the Holy Spirit who is the soul of the believing community. These theocentrists are still adhering to the old theism that regards it impertinent to meddle in matters that supposedly make no sense. They start with a philosophical postulate of an imperishable God who would never incarnate a finite human mortal.

The biblical narrative tells the gospel as the history of Jesus the Son in relation to his Father and of their relation to their common Spirit. To do justice to this story, the theology of the church had to develop a trinitarian concept of God. Confronted by three persons in the drama of salvation, theology had to ask about the nature of their unity. The reverse method of starting with the assumption of unity in the interest of a strict monotheism—whether of Jewish, Greek, or Roman provenance—led to the Arian and Sabellian heresies. Because the Western Latin tradition began with the assumption of unity and then proceeded to inquire into the Trinity, it has produced an unstable record on the Trinity that has threatened to unravel into unitarianism with its accompanying Arian Christology, in which Christ is something lower than God. The new trinitarians break with this tradition and resume contact with the Greek patristic tradition that begins with the three persons and then goes on to ask about their unity.

The narrative of the gospel proceeds to speak of God in human terms. It identifies the living God with the crucified Jesus of Nazareth and thus reveals the life of the crucified God. God is never more divine than when he becomes human and never more self-revealing in his true essence, love, than in the death and resurrection of Jesus. The new theocentric pluralists dismiss the incarnational kenosis of God as a myth full of mischief. They bear the spirit of the philosopher Spinoza, who held that God is not permitted to be human and that God and humanity are mutually exclusive. He wrote: "The doctrines added by certain churches, such as that God took on himself human nature, I have expressly said that I do not understand; in fact, to speak the truth, they seem to me no less absurd than would a statement that a circle had taken on itself the nature of a square."[24] In the mouth of a Christian theologian, the statement would be troublesome. Spinoza, however, was neither a Christian nor a theologian; he was a Jew and a philosopher. The confession of the Trinity is a mystery of faith and not a postulate of metaphysical reason.

In Jesus Christ, God has entered into the temporal structure of our world and history. The eternal Word of God has become human flesh. God has become enmeshed in history; as Jüngel puts it, "entangled in stories."[25] The humanity of God can best be talked about in narrative form. Hegel tried to translate the stories into an absolute philosophy, to convert the earthly symbols of theology into the heavenly concepts of an absolute philosophy. Even if we do not intend to go that far with Hegel, his concepts are not useless. Hegel helped to show that God is not a prisoner of his own being, trapped in timeless immutability, unable to experience change through relationships with another. Indeed, in God there is real otherness; he empties himself into one that is other, through whom he reveals and manifests himself. That in itself is a necessary condition of love. Mutuality and relationship belong to the eternal dynamics of love. God does not only love, but God *is* love. In Jesus Christ, the love of God expresses itself in the extremity of death; death is put to death, and reconciliation occurs through the negation of negation. In such a way, Hegel's dialectics have provided the new trinitarians, including Barth and Rahner, with a conceptual apparatus more useful to the gospel than the old theistic metaphysics that viewed the incarnation as an unthinkable thought. For Hegel, to say that the infinite can encompass the finite (*infinitum capax finiti*) is even metaphysically true. The kenosis, suffering, and death of Jesus are the expression of the fullness of God's love and, therefore, not a divine self-contradiction.

God in Christ was loving the world with the very same love that constitutes his being as a communion of reciprocal relations. God appears in history in the way he eternally is; otherwise, we could not be sure that in the history of Jesus we

are dealing with God himself. There is an ontological correspondence between the internal relations of Father, Son, and
Holy Spirit and the outward (*ad extra*) fulfillment of those relations. Pannenberg puts it this way:

> For the love with which the Father loved the Son and which the
> Son reciprocates is also the love through which God loved the world
> and the love which, through the Holy Spirit, is poured out into the
> hearts of believers, that they might be one with God and with one
> another, just as the Father is one with the Son and the Son with the
> Father. . . . So that phrase "God is love" is to be understood as the
> comprehensive expression of the trinitarian fellowship of Father,
> Son, and Spirit.[26]

The structure of God's love which we receive through
Christ in the Spirit is trinitarian through and through.

History is key to the logic of such trinitarian thinking. God's
being in himself and his coming in history are not two separate
trinities. That would render one or the other redundant. The
subtitle of one of Jüngel's books is *Gottes Sein ist im Werden*
(God's Being Is in Becoming). God's being as God and what he
becomes in history through the salvation-historical workings
of the Son and the Spirit are one and the same. What happened
to Jesus is what happens to God. The death of Jesus is an event
to be told in the biography of God.

Church Unity and Mission

I expect that some—perhaps even many—may be asking what
this emphasis on Trinity has to do with the topic at hand, namely,
with the church's unity and mission. Why cannot we simply
get on with the business of ecumenical cooperation for common
witness? As a Lutheran theologian, I am committed to the answer of article seven of the Augsburg Confession that for the
true unity of the church it is sufficient, but also necessary, that
we agree on the truth of the gospel. To put it bluntly, we do
not want to cooperate in joint witness with those who trumpet
a different gospel. This was also the spirit of the apostle Paul,
who admonished the Galatians who were "turning to a different
gospel" that "if anyone proclaims to you a gospel contrary to
what you received, let that one be accursed!" (1:6, 9). Why
should we be any less concerned?

The doctrine of the Trinity is the solid declaration of the gospel of Jesus Christ; it is not a product of speculation that has little or nothing to do with salvation. Its function is to tell every generation of Christians which gospel they are to believe, teach, and confess. The Athanasian Creed put the matter more strongly perhaps than I am prepared to do: "Whoever wants to be saved should think thus about the Trinity." I am not talking about the necessity of believing the dogma of the Trinity in every jot and tittle to be saved. I am talking about the necessity of the church to use the doctrine of the Trinity to discriminate between the truth of the gospel and all its fashionable rivals within and outside the churches.

We need the truth of the Trinity to measure what we say throughout the whole of theology, to rescue it from its "splendid isolation." The Trinity may be for us a model for our thinking about the unity of the church. Christians frequently tend to think of the unity of the church in monarchical terms. Ignatius formulated this principle: one bishop, one church. Just as God was thought to be essentially a monarch, so there must be a corresponding monarch in the church. The monarchical episcopate was the governing model of church unity for ages, and to imagine anything else is still difficult. In the Roman Catholic Church, the monarchical episcopate achieved its heightened expression in the dogma of papal supremacy and infallibility. The oneness of the office legitimates the oneness of the church.

The social-historical construction of the Trinity may open up an alternative way of conceiving unity. Perhaps monotheistic monarchianism not only dominates the doctrine of God but also undergirds the patriarchal system of human relationships. It may lie at the root of the religion of patriarchy. Images of authority and unity are social constructions. If the Christian doctrine of the Trinity were taken seriously, would it not help us to make a break with the kind of radical monotheism that guarantees the monarchical model of church unity? Might there not be a trinitarian starting point for rethinking church unity as a communion of believers emancipated by the gospel?

The unity of the church is based on the Trinity, and according to Eph 4:4-6: "There is one body and one Spirit . . . one Lord, one faith, one baptism, one God and Father of us all." St. Cyprian stated that the church is "a people brought into

unity from the unity of the Father, the Son and the Holy Spirit."[27] The unity of the church is a prefigurement of the unity of humankind that God is working to bring about. The ecumenical movement is surely a part of that plan. Unity is the perennial question of humanity. In the ultimate ground of all reality in the Trinity, we do not find a unity in which multiplicity disappears into the dark night of undifferentiated nothingness. Rather, we find a unity which presupposes and gives ultimate value to relationship, reciprocity, and mutuality between members in a loving communion of equals.

The origin of the church is rooted in God's plan for the salvation of the world. Christianity is not essentially a religious expression of a particular culture. It can be shown to be that, of course, from a sociological perspective. The church, however, understands itself to be a people elected to serve the triune God for the benefit of all people. It does this primarily by bringing the good news of salvation in Jesus Christ to all the nations. That is its mission; yet, more profoundly, it is the mission of the triune God. The church does not move God around the world; God moves the church around the world through the ongoing activities of all three persons of the Trinity. Augustine's trinitarian formula that the outward works of the Trinity are undivided (*opera Trinitatis ad extra indivisa sunt*) is unacceptable, as unacceptable as the ancient theological opinion that any one of the three persons of the Trinity could just as well have become incarnate. Acceptance of such an opinion would dissolve the differentiated works of the three persons whose identities are established precisely through their reciprocal relations.

The sending of the church to the world is a continuation of the Father's sending of the Son and the Spirit. These sending operations aim to awaken faith, to baptize, and to start new communities of discipleship. The Holy Spirit leads the church to open new fields of mission and to continue the apostolic history that began at Pentecost in Jerusalem. At the beginning, the church was nothing else than the mission of the gospel driven onward by the Spirit. As Robert Jenson says so aptly: "the first gatherings of believers were gatherings of missionaries."[28] If we surrender this missionary identity of the church, we will be left to serve some other gods, perhaps the pagan gods of blood and soil, the gods of our race, or land, or class, or gender. We are commissioned to speak in the name of the triune God. We are authorized to speak *to* this God in worship, to speak *for* this God in proclamation, and to speak *about* this God in theology. Apart from the God of the gospel, our talk will revolve around someone else. The Bible calls this idolatry.

Should the church today continue to evangelize the nations in the name of the triune God? That is basically the same question as: Should the church continue to be the church? The church is constituted by the structure of the trinitarian mission of God in the history of salvation. The church is the eschatological creation of God's Word serving to unite all humankind. Each person integrated into the Christian community, the body of Christ, is baptized into the triune name. Each person, together with the entire body of which he or she is a member, exists within the context of the trinitarian history of God's mission. They are nourished at the Lord's Table, whose eucharistic liturgy is intertwined with the trinitarian naming of God. The Father is praised; the Son is remembered; the Spirit is invoked. As Jenson says: "So obtrusive is this structure that in the most ancient church the Thanksgiving was often understood as an act *of* the Trinity: as praise to the Father, offered with the Son and the Spirit."[29]

A church that gathers all its members around the Word and the sacraments will not be confused about whether the Lord's commission to evangelize the nations is still valid. Any church that forgets this has entered into self-contradiction and apostasy. The church's call to mission is a matter of life and death; it goes to the heart of the question whether to be or not to be truly the church. To question the permanent validity of the church's call to mission is to tear it out of its proper trinitarian and christological framework. I have tried to overcome such confusion by emphasizing that the church's mission to all the nations is a participation in the works of the triune God.

The Trinity as ground and motive for ecumenism and mission has its clear center in Christ, but its circumference is as wide as creation. The Trinity provides us with the most comprehensive framework for understanding the place of the church in world history, to interpret the forces of secularization, science, and technology, to motivate concern and loving care for the earth, to stimulate the dialogue between the religions, and to promote international trends toward a peaceful world that will embrace justice and freedom. Trinitarian theology calls the church to the front lines of mission that will distinguish but refuse to separate two dimensions of mission. If one is not accustomed to using Luther's distinction between two kingdoms, one is free to choose a different image. Moltmann identifies these two dimensions when he speaks of a quantitative and a qualitative aspect of mission: The quantitative mission is the spread of the gospel to the ends of the earth, and that must always continue. The qualitative mission aims to influence the conditions under which people live, "directed towards an alteration of the whole atmosphere of life."[30] Within a trinitarian framework, the church understands itself to be driven by the Spirit in every direction and into every dimension of life; but the church always knows that its center and criterion are given in the gospel. The task of the Spirit is to make the person and work of Christ present in the world, to bring history to its goal in the kingdom of God when, in the end, God will be all in all.

[7]

God the Creator
Orders Public Life

AN RULER, the Dutch theologian, said in one of his books that sex, politics, and religion are the only subjects worth talking about. Luther would have agreed, because these concerns happen to coincide with his own threefold division of the orders of creation: *status economicus, status politicus,* and *status ecclesiasticus.* Luther collapsed sexual identity and family status into the economic order because the household, in the broadest sense, was the basic sphere in which people secured all the necessities of livelihood. I will leave aside the question whether Luther ever used the expression *Schöpfungsordnungen* in reference to the orders.[1] Other expressions, however, were used and meant the same thing or something similar, expressions such as *ordo, ordo divina, ordo naturalis, ordinatio, ordinatio divina, creatura Dei, weltliches Regiment, potestas ordinata,* to mention a few.[2] Surely those Lutherans who developed an explicit theology of the orders of creation consciously drew their basic ideas from Luther, but I am not specifically addressing here the question of how much of that theology can be found in Luther's works as such. Rather, I am attending to the most recent segment of Lutheran theological history.

The Orders of Creation Revisited

The modern form of the doctrine of the orders of creation goes back to nineteenth-century German Lutheranism. Adolf von

Harless is usually credited with the reaffirmation of a theology of orders. He preferred to speak, however, not so much of the orders of creation (*Schöpfungsordnungen*) but of the orders of the Creator (*Schöpferordnungen*).[3] The point of this doctrine is to affirm that Christians like all other human beings exist in a framework of universal structures that are there prior to and apart from the fact that Christians believe in Christ and belong to his Church. God has placed all human beings in particular structures of existence—such as nationality, race, sexual identity, family, work, government—that in some form or other are simply givens of creaturely existence. The law and commandments of God are revealed through these common created morphological structures of human existence and function apart from and in tension with the special revelation of God in the gospel of Jesus Christ. This means that there is a double revelation of God. This duality permeates the whole system of theological categories and lies at the base of the familiar distinctions made, for example, between God hidden and God revealed (*Deus absconditus et Deus revelatus*), creation and redemption, law and gospel, the two kingdoms, the two aeons, the old ego and the new, and the concept of *simul iustus et peccator* (righteous yet sinful) that is the double subjectivity of every believer.

Karl Barth severely criticized these distinctions. Instead, he developed a theology of the one Word of God from which all structures, orders, commandments, and ethical norms for Christian living in the world must be derived. I call this the soteriological captivity of creation, because it succeeds in emptying the world of its own meaning as a realm of divine governance and human involvement prior to and apart from the biblical story of salvation culminating in Christ. I believe we need to break this one Word of God in two and restore the validity of the distinction for the sake of the integrity of the gospel.

I wish to say just a word about the timeliness of this move for the church today. If the world is void of God's presence and activity apart from the gospel, this means that Christians are called upon to fill it up. That is a hard job, so the churches must expend every effort to fill the void.[4] If the churches bear the only Word of God there is, if only this Word establishes the reality and meaning of everything going on in the world—its politics, economics, and cultural life—no wonder that the churches have become overexuberant. This accounts for the fact that the churches around the world have politicized themselves from the inside out and exhausted themselves by trying to tell the world what to do, including issuing directives for social and political action. This might be a good thing if it would work, but it does not. Worse yet, and more to the point of my concern, is that the translation of the one Word of God into direct social and political rhetoric about praxis means that the churches neglect to proclaim the message for which they have sole responsibility, which constitutes their specific raison d'être and which no other agency in the world is called on or competent to do; and that message is the eternal gospel of Holy Scripture that has the power to make people wise unto salvation through faith in Christ Jesus (2 Tim 3:15).

The heyday of the neo-Lutheran theology of the orders of creation goes back to Germany in the 1930s when an outpouring of books and articles on the subject occurred. Werner Elert, Paul Althaus, Walther Künneth, and Friedrich Gogarten wrote extensively. I should also include Emil Brunner, who, though not a Lutheran, wrote several books on the orders of creation (two examples: *The Divine Imperative,* the English title for *Das Gebot und die Ordnungen* [1932]; and *Justice and the Social Order,* a translation of *Gerechtigkeit* [1943]). About Brunner's effort Kart Barth wrote:

> I do not fully understand the intention and spirit of the book. . . . What I do not understand is from what source and in what way Brunner claims to know these orders. . . . We cannot help feeling that at the root of his conception of "orders" there lies something akin to the familiar notion of a *lex naturae* [natural law] which is immanent in reality and inscribed upon the heart of man, so that it is directly known to him. But does not this mean that there is not only a second (or first) revelation of God before and beside that of the Word of His grace, but also a second (or first) knowledge of God beside that of this Word of grace?[5]

Karl Barth's relentless attack on natural theology motivates his rejection of the orders of creation because of their family resemblance to the idea of natural law. The resemblance exists because people do not need to know Jesus Christ to have some knowledge of what is right and good through the law of God's creation and conscience, which "have been understood and seen through the things he has made" (Rom 1:20). Despite all the affinity between the Thomist-Aristotelian theory of natural law and the Lutheran theology of the orders of creation, we will also need to observe their fundamental difference, which Barth's criticism blurs.

A rehabilitation of the orders of creation must take into account its weaknesses and the validity of many of the criticisms levelled against it. A major criticism is that the whole notion of orders suffers from a static picture of creation.[6] These fundamental orders seem to have a supralapsarian essence outside of history, with all the markings of a mythological primeval time. This theology of orders fails to appreciate that we live inescapably in the changing structures of historical development. Thus Wolfhart Pannenberg rightly asks: "But are there really ordinances which constitute equally all forms of society that have developed in history, ordinances whose historical expressions are merely variants? Is not each concrete form of society thoroughly determined by its history?"[7] Helmut Thielicke has taken this criticism seriously in his *Theological Ethics* when he speaks of the various structures of our common life (such as the state, law, economics, etc.) as orders of history rather than as orders of creation and then presents them in an infralapsarian way as "orders of the divine patience, given because of our 'hardness of heart' (Matt 19:8)."[8]

The infusion of historical relativity into the orders can also break their linkage to an ethical conservatism that is always standing against every revolutionary development and thus denying the freedom of God to do a new thing or two in the world. If the world were pictured not as an eternal cosmos but as a historical process, then the orders would not be placed in a timeless realm above and beyond history. Just as Lutheran theology criticized natural law on account of its abstract, formalistic, and unhistorical conception of human nature, so also the idea of a definite constellation of fixed orders of life seems to be nearly as remote from the dynamic character of historical development. Acknowledging the historicity of the command of God addressing all people in the common associations of life should at least discourage every ideological absolutization of transient formations of life.

Furthermore, the idea of the orders of creation must be qualified both by the fact that the original creation has been distorted by the fall into a universal condition of rebellion against God's design for the world and the fact that the Christian faith longs for the restoration and fulfillment of creation through the history of God's redemption in Jesus Christ. For this reason, some Lutheran theologians prefer to speak of orders of preservation by taking into account what God is doing to sustain the world under the conditions of sin and even using in themselves sin-laden means, such as war and capital punishment, to fight against still more serious attacks on the goodness of God's creation. God's preserving creativity is an expression of the continuing creativity of God until God's final purpose for the world reaches its completion in the eschaton.

A Brief Theological Sketch

The Barthian attack on the orders of creation was so devastating that some Lutherans veered radically to the other extreme of situation ethics.[9] After World War II, theology was awash in such an existentialist deconstruction of ontology, ethical norms, nomological principles, and traditional values that Christian moral instruction ceased almost entirely. The churches have not yet recovered from the evacuation of serious moral discourse. We have lost our way in a labyrinthine antinomianism which leaves it up to each individual to intuit his or her way out of a moral crisis. In the ethical situation, Christians are told to rely on what the Spirit nudges them to do on the spur of the existential moment,[10] and according to Kinsey that amounts to doing pretty much what everybody else is doing. I am afraid that this Kinseyesque approach to moral questions has now been adopted by the churches, so that taking samples from a cross-section of the population is thought to be the way to discover God's will on any issue. The pluralism and relativism built into this sociological method of approach are the latest substitutes for the theology of law and the orders of creation that framed the ethical discussions of our church in the past. We are mired in a moral marshland; we have no firm ground under our feet. Having wallowed around in this swamp long enough, I think it's time to look back to the sturdier traditions of our own Lutheran heritage and, rather than condemn or forget them, seek to recuperate and revise them. I will try to do a little of that now in a brief sketch of a theology of the orders of creation.

Definition. The orders of creation are the common structures of human existence, the indispensable conditions of the possibility of social life. Through these structures human beings are bound to each other in various relationships and mutual service. Luther said: "You will always be in a station. You are either a husband, wife, son, daughter, servant, or maid."[11] "Saint Peter says that the graces and gifts of God are not all of one kind, but various. And each one is to realize what his own are and use them so that he may be of use to others. What a fine thing it would be if everyone took care of his own, while at the same time thereby serving his neighbor. So they would journey amicably together on the right road to heaven."[12]

Reason. The orders of creation are givens that can be experienced and recognized by common human reason apart from faith and theology; so Luther could say: "God does not have to have Christians as magistrates; it is not necessary, therefore, that the ruler be a saint; he does not need to be a Christian in order to rule, it is sufficient that he possess reason."[13] Everyone participates in some way in the political, economic, and familial systems of society and is called upon to contribute to each of them in the service of others.

Faith. Those who believe in God acknowledge the common structures of human existence as the creation of God. Reason can discern the orders; only faith can read them as the creative activity of God. Faith is the presupposition of a theology of the orders of creation. By faith we confess that God has created us and all that exists, which is something quite different from claiming to know that once upon a time in the far distant past God created the very same structures in which we now participate. The confession of creation must be set free from its bondage to the myth of protological beginnings when that means to read the first eleven chapters of Genesis in a literal-historical manner.

Sin and Death. We may speak of the fundamental universal structures of life as orders of creation because God continues to create these possibilities of existence in spite of the fact that we live in a world of sin and death. The confession that we are creatures of God is coupled with the confession that we are the children of Adam and Eve and, therefore, fallen and sinful members of the human race. We live in the tension between the dignity of creation and the dis-grace of sin, between the joy of being God's creatures and the shame of perverting this status. The orders of creation are subject to the conditions of sin and death; nevertheless, they are still the object of God's continuing and present activity of creating, as Luther so clearly stressed. God did not create once upon a time and then let things run their course, as the deists maintained. Every act of preservation on this side of sin and death is still an act of ongoing creation. Thus, we have a right to speak of the orders of creation in the interim between the fall and the final consummation, with the proviso that there are no orders of creation that are not affected by the powers of sin and death.

Conscience. The orders of creation are the media through which the command of God addresses the conscience of all human beings. God speaks the law through the structures of creation and impinges on the human conscience. Women experience the gift and task of motherhood immediately within their consciences once they become mothers. Spanning the entire spectrum of creation, whether in terms of sex, politics, or religion, God is speaking through the law written on human hearts, with their consciences picking up the signals, either accusing or excusing them, until that day when God will finally judge all things by the criterion of Jesus Christ (Rom 1:15-16). There are two steps here: God speaks the law through the ordinary things of daily life; but his extraordinary Word is spoken from the endtime through Jesus Christ, who fulfills and transcends the law of creation. Is it not true that the second table of the law is known throughout the world and embodies "knowledge and truth" (Rom 2:20) but that only the biblical revelation of the Creator grounds them more deeply in the first commandment and the first table of the law?

Eschatology. Faith in Jesus Christ places all the orders of creation under the spotlight of the eschatological kingdom and rule of God. This means that the orders are relativized and subject to the conditions of historical life. They cannot evolve into a state of perfection, thus establishing the kingdom of God. No marrying or giving in marriage exists in the kingdom of

God (Matt 22:30) and no law and force, because everything will give way to the service of love. The orders pertain to this world of sin and death, and so they will cease when the kingdom comes. As such they are provisional and penultimate. Thus Luther could say that the exercise of power by the authorities of law and government constitutes the "alien work" of God, not his "proper work." They are the work of the "left hand of God."

Civil Righteousness. Just as the orders of creation cannot be equated with the kingdom of God, so also they must not be separated from the coming kingdom. God acts through the orders to preserve the world and its history until the kingdom comes. Luther saw that the task of government was to keep the peace so that God could gather his people through the preaching of the gospel. That is the political function of the orders. The orders are also a school in which all citizens are educated to care for each other, to do their duties, even against their egoistic drives, and to use their "liberty and ability to achieve civil righteousness," as article 17 of the Apology of the Augsburg Confession puts it. Such civil righteousness is not the same as spiritual righteousness, namely, the true pure love that only the Holy Spirit can work in our hearts against the impulses of the flesh. Between these two types of righteousness stands the radical event of conversion, the new birth, which no amount of good thinking, willing, or feeling can bring about. It is the miracle of grace, communicated through the Word in the power of the Spirit. This summons to civil righteousness may be called the pedagogical function of the orders.

Third Use of the Law. There has been a continuing debate in Lutheran theology about the third use of the law. However one may come down on that, I would agree with Paul Althaus that there is a third function of the orders in relation to the kingdom of God, and that is the symbolical function.[14] The liberty, peace, and justice for which we strive in our worldly existence may be seen as parables of the kingdom. Although they do not establish the kingdom, they may be seen as signs and anticipations of the eternal *shalom* for which the whole creation longs and waits.

The Two Tables of the Law. God is the Lord of life and therefore sets limits to the demands which the orders place upon us. None of the orders may be so absolutized as to abolish the others. Our loyalties to state, ethnic group, vocation, or family are all valid in their own way, and none should dominate all the others. "Therefore what God has joined together, let no one separate" (Matt 19:6). All the claims and commandments of the second table of the law are limited by the freedom and sovereignty of God in the first table of the law; so Jesus could say: "Whoever comes to me and does not hate father and mother, wife and children, brothers and sisters, yes, and even life itself, cannot be my disciple" (Luke 14:26). The law that is mediated through the orders is not unconditional. It is always subject to Peter's principle: "We must obey God rather than any human authority" (Acts 5:29). To observe the proper dialectic between the first and the second tables of the law, between what we owe to God alone and what we owe to our fellow human beings, is always a fine art.

Service. God continues to order the natural life of humanity by means of the concrete historical structures that actually impinge on our existence—the particular systems of government, economics, and family life that frame our life. No ideal state exists, no ideal marriage, no ideal economic system—as though God's Word should be equated with some abstract ideal structures of life. We are summoned to divine obedience and neighborly service within the framework of concrete human historical structures, as questionable and ambiguous as they always are. We cannot wait for the right time and place to obey God and serve our neighbors, but we are not called to submit uncritically to the status quo. Every structure of life must be examined to see if it measures up to God's intention for it, whether its current form works for the common good in the service of justice, liberty, and community.

Ambiguity. The concept of ambiguity is useful to express that the orders of creation are good as created by God and yet permeated by the law of sin and death. We live on this side of Eden in a fallen world in which demonic forces are intertwined with structures of divine preservation. The same structures of life work both good and evil. Divine and demonic powers struggle for control; at times, the battle seems to tilt in favor of the one side over the other. The history of theology is replete with examples of denial of this hard truth that the world is permeated

127

with divine-demonic ambiguity. Types of monistic idealism deny the reality of the demonic, of Satan. The evil that strikes us is not real; it is only one chord struck in the wonderful melody of life as seen from a higher perspective. Death is only a passing phase of the grand march of the Spirit in the unfolding epic of cosmic evolution. Death is actually only a means to life. The dialectics of idealism denies the reality of sin and evil, the demonic, and the satanic forces penetrating all the structures of life. On the other hand, there are the old and new forms of Manichaean dualism that surrender the structures of this life to the devil and deny that they come from the benevolent hand of God. The world is going to hell in a handbasket, some say. Will God allow it? The truth is that life in all of its dimensions occurs under the law of ambiguity. We experience it as a blessing and as a curse, sometimes predominantly one more than the other, but never exclusively one without the other.

Bondage. The ambiguity of life in the tension between the blessing of creation and the curse of death means that all of our actions participate in this ambiguity. We cannot obey God without at the same time giving the devil his due. The ambiguity does not lie merely on the subjective side, in the person. Luther rightly stressed that the person is always a sinner, whose will is in bondage; but so are the structures in bondage, and no matter what one does with the best of intentions, something evil comes of it. That is the dreadful truth about our ambiguous existence. Luther saw the wrath of God at work when he observed that we as sinners cannot fulfill any of God's commands without at the same time entrapping ourselves in sin. God's wrath is poured out upon humanity because by the very zeal we exert to do our duty and excel in our vocation, we contribute to the dynamics of sin and death in the world. Order and chaos, good and evil, blessing and curse, and moral man and immoral society remain so intermixed that many are inclined to doubt that God is Lord of this world, and they sink into skepticism and nihilism.

Forgiveness. Such despair in the face of the universal and radical human predicament can only be overcome through the gospel, which announces forgiveness of sins and redemption of life under the conditions of this ambiguous world chained by sin and death. The gospel proclaims the victory of Jesus Christ over sin, death, and the power of Satan and inaugurates hope that ultimately and fundamentally God will establish his rule over all his enemies and ours. The gospel declares that we receive forgiveness under the conditions of life within the framework of the orders; it does not beckon us to forsake them and escape into a make-believe world of sinless perfectionism. That was the error of monasticism that Luther challenged.

Redemption. The message of the gospel is not only for-giveness but also redemption from the power of death and the demonic forces at work in history. The crucified and risen Jesus Christ has defeated Satan and death. Colossians 2:15 states: "He disarmed the rulers and authorities and made a public example of them, triumphing over them in it." The dynamics of death and the demonic powers have been defeated and put to death in the cross and resurrection of Jesus Christ. That is the gospel—the Christ event. This victory, however, is not manifest in all reality. Death has been defeated, and still people die. We live between the times. In Christ the ambiguity of creation and the fall under the dominion of death and Satan has been overcome, but the rest of creation waits for the final victory until the eschaton.

Freedom. The freedom of the Christian comes through faith in the victory of Jesus Christ. It is a derived and participatory freedom. By the assurance of forgiveness, Christians are called called to do battle against the forces of sin and death that ef-fectively penetrate the orders of creation, and they are free to continue struggling and suffering within them, always seeking to do God's will. Although only death will liberate us from sin, we are already free to fight against its effects in public and personal life, in many little moral decisions made from day to day.

The Implications for the Church and Society

We do not live in a theocracy, so we cannot expect that God's work and rule in the public orders of life will be mediated by a hierarchy of priests, preachers, or prelates. We will not return to the society of ancient Israel, medieval Europe, Calvin's Ge-neva, or modern Iran. We cannot, therefore, entertain the idea that God orders public life through laws and directives coming from organized religion or the institutional church and bearing on the political, economic, and social life of the people. Nor is Jesus Christ some kind of ayatollah who communicates a blueprint of an ideal society and calls upon his believers to make laws, pronounce judgment, and execute his will in the public spheres. For this reason also we have rejected the Barthian christocratic scheme: it starts from the one Word of God, Jesus Christ, then moves centrifugally from the inside out, from the inner circle of believers to the wider human community. If the community of believers were to coincide with the community of citizens, this might be a plausible scheme. Whenever this is not the case, the believers' vision of society must be imposed on the larger number of unbelievers through force. The theocratic and the christocratic ways of representing the divine will for the public orders are both thoroughly reprehensible, although they are always temptations for true believers who deplore the secularization of life and wish to put God back into the naked public square. We must, therefore, oppose the current efforts to re-Christianize the public orders and to legislate the will of the churched upon the unchurched as though we have a special revelation from Christ for the political and social conditions of life today.

I believe that Lutherans today should be in the best position to deal with the challenges of a pluralistic secular society. The doctrine of the orders of creation goes hand in glove with the doctrine of the two kingdoms. This means that the church and its members have a double identity. As members of the church they are concerned with the gospel, but the God of the gospel is also the God of the law at work in the secular realm where the churched and the unchurched share a common ground. This scheme allows that the rule of God in the public orders is not primarily in the hands of believers but is communicated to all persons through the natural orders and can be grasped through conscience and moral reason. No secular world exists in which God is dead, no empty world into which believers have to introduce the law of God for the first time. God is at work through his ongoing creativity and through the law that orders life in the world. The law is an instrument of divine activity and confronts all persons in their actual empirical existence. No sphere of life exists where God is not active through the law that impinges on the human conscience. God is universally present as the pressure that drives people to do justice even when they are not just, to earn a living for their families even when they are lazy, to give to others their due even though they are filled with selfish desires. Life could not go on for a minute without the pressures that God exerts behind the back of every individual. We experience God's law as the driving force behind the demands that human beings impose on each other as they live in community. The criterion that measures which demands are legitimate and have God as their anonymous author is available to all people in the ideal of justice. What is justice? The core of justice in all times and places is care for the neighbor. The force required to administer justice through law is the strange work (*opus alienum*) of love in public life. The whole law is summarized in the commandment: "You shall love your neighbor as yourself" (Matt 19:19). A particular law, therefore, is just when functioning in the care of human beings, suppressing evil deeds, and rewarding the good.

Luther spoke of the orders of creation, family, state, work, as the masks of God (*larvae Dei*), masks of the hidden living God. Gustaf Wingren speaks of the presence of God incognito in the demands we meet in daily life.[15] No life is free of the pressures that God exerts, pressures arising from within the depth of our being and bearing down upon us through the presence of others. Psalm 139:1-8 expresses this conviction in beautiful words:

O LORD, you have searched me and known me.
You know when I sit down and when I rise up;
  you discern my thoughts from far away.
You search out my path and my lying down,
  and are acquainted with all my ways.
Even before a word is on my tongue,
  O LORD, you know it completely.
You hem me in, behind and before,
  and lay your hand upon me.
Such knowledge is too wonderful for me;
  it is so high that I cannot attain it.
Where can I go from your spirit?
  Or where can I flee from your presence?
If I ascend to heaven, you are there;
  if I make my bed in Sheol, you art there . . .

We do not expect salvation from what God is doing in the kingdom of the left hand. Our actions to promote peace, justice, and liberation are not on the same plane as the qualitatively other kingdom which God has brought from beyond our world of possibilities through Jesus Christ. The eschatological kingdom of God in the ministry of Christ and his church does not come about through the politics of this world, which always and necessarily involve compulsion and violence. "My kingdom is not from this world. If my kingdom were from this world, my followers would be fighting. . . . my kingdom is not from here" (John 18:36).

The task of the Christian church is to preach Christ and all that pertains to God's eschatological message of salvation that comes solely through Christ. The church understands itself to be the first heirs of this kingdom through faith alone, worked by the power of the Holy Spirit through the means of grace, the Word and sacraments. If this were all that God were doing in the world, we would have no need for a doctrine of two kingdoms. God works, however, through such worldly means as politics, economics, family life, and so forth; and God works differently through these natural orders of life. Therein lies the essence of the necessary distinction between the two kingdoms of God. Any church or theology that dismisses this distinction promotes the most pernicious things in both the church and the world. Either the content of the gospel as eternal salvation is reduced to a social message to ameliorate the conditions of life in this world or it is equated with the loftiest wisdom of philosophy and heroic examples of moral achievement. Thus Jesus is placed roughly on the par with Plato, Confucius, Marx, and others. The eternal peace of humanity with God, received by faith on account of Christ's victory over sin, death, and the power of Satan, is dismissed as pie in the sky in exchange for the various approximations of peace and happiness that, in good times, this world also knows about and experiences. To distinguish eternal peace from earthly peace, eternal salvation from this-worldly liberation, and social justice from the righteousness of faith does not diminish or discredit the earthly social-historical dimensions of what is true and good and beautiful. These things are also works of God in his ongoing ordering of creation. One kingdom does not need to be played off against the other. Both are valid in their own way under the twofold activity of the living God.

The church and its members have a special and exclusive calling to be witnesses of God's promise of eternal salvation through faith in Jesus Christ. No other structure in the whole wide world can be called on to promise eternal salvation; and when such totalitarian claims are made in the name of some nation, race, social class, religion, or ideology, the church must fight such idolatry and blasphemy with all its means of persuasion, even if that means going to the cross of martyrdom. Such Christian exclusiveness is under heavy attack these days, not only from the side of the world as one might expect but from within the church itself, its various councils, bureaucracies, and theologies. It is a fifth-column movement, a Quisling conspiracy against the gospel itself, a subversion of Christianity from within broad segments of church leadership.

If we confuse liberation movements with eternal salvation, we convert the gospel into an ideological promotion of political and social transformation. The doctrine of the two kingdoms guards us from this confusion. Whoever believes in the gospel of Jesus Christ is a new creation, not just anyone in the vanguard of political and social liberation movements. We cannot expect too much from the orders of creation in a fallen world. That would only lead either to fanaticism and revolutionary violence or to despair and disillusionment. We have seen examples in our lifetime of persons imbued with revolutionary fervor in their youth who become cynical opportunists in their maturity. If they cannot change the system for the future good of everyone, they settle for what it can presently do for themselves.

If the Lutheran confessing movement has stood for anything, it has waged war against works-righteousness in the name of the gospel, but that is the only kind of righteousness we can expect from the most virtuous accomplishments in the orders of public life. The righteousness of Christ available through faith alone is something totally other. It is totally a gift from God, received freely through faith apart from the works of the law. If you play by the rules of the game in the orders of creation, you may win prizes commensurate with your efforts, but all that will do nothing to secure your eternal peace with God.

I have argued that we need to rehabilitate the doctrine of the orders of creation so that we will not legalize the gospel to fill the structures of public life. God is already at work there through the law of creation that is other than the gospel. We do not have to be Christians to read and understand this law, but only baptized believers know the gospel of Jesus Christ in the fullest sense. Christians and non-Christians are on the same footing in the orders of creation, subject to the same criteria and judged by the same standards. The grace of God in Jesus Christ will not buy out a failing business. Conversely, the best government or social system in the world cannot forgive sin, overcome death, or secure eternal salvation. That is what the gospel does, and it is ultimately for the sake of its integrity and uniqueness that we need to rehabilitate the old Lutheran doctrine of the orders of creation.

Notes

Introduction: Question Mark—Exclamation Point

1. See Paul F. Knitter, *No Other Name? A Critical Survey of Christian Attitudes toward the World Religions* (Maryknoll, N.Y.: Orbis Books, 1985).

2. See John Hick and Paul F. Knitter, eds., *The Myth of Christian Uniqueness: Toward a Pluralistic Theology of Religions* (Maryknoll, N.Y.: Orbis Books, 1988).

3. Karl Rahner, "Anonymous Christianity and the Missionary Task of the Church," in vol. 12 of *Theological Investigations* (New York: Seabury Press, 1974), 161–78.

4. See my recent book, *Justification: The Article by which the Church Stands or Falls* (Minneapolis: Fortress Press, 1990).

5. This eschatological motif was developed in two of my books on missiology: *The Flaming Center: A Theology of the Christian Mission* (Philadelphia: Fortress Press, 1977), and *The Apostolic Imperative: Nature and Aim of the Church's Mission and Ministry* (Minneapolis: Augsburg Publishing House, 1985).

6. Karl Rahner, *The Trinity*, trans. Joseph Donceel (New York: Herder and Herder, 1970), 22.

7. Knitter, *No Other Name?* 104.

8. An example of this tendency is the book by Lee Snook, *The Anonymous Christ* (Minneapolis: Augsburg Publishing House, 1986).

Chapter 1: American Protestantism Lacks a Reformation

1. Dietrich Bonhoeffer, "Protestantismus ohne Reformation," in *Gesammelte Schriften,* ed. Eberhard Bethge (Munich: Chr. Kaiser Verlag, 1958), 323–54.

2. Ibid., 325.

3. Ibid., 352, 354.

4. Ibid., 353–54.

5. H. Richard Niebuhr, *The Kingdom of God in America* (New York: Harper and Brothers, 1937), 150.

6. Allan Bloom, *The Closing of the American Mind* (New York: Simon and Schuster, 1987), 25, 26.

7. Jeffrey Stout, *Ethics After Babel: The Language of Morals and Their Discontents* (Boston: Beacon Press, 1988), 163.

8. See James M. Gustafson, vol. 1 of *Ethics from a Theocentric Perspective* (Chicago: University of Chicago Press, 1981).

9. Ibid., 270.

10. Stout, *Ethics after Babel,* 171.

11. Gustafson, *Ethics from a Theocentric Perspective,* 310.

12. Ibid., 276.

13. Hick and Knitter, *The Myth of Christian Uniqueness.*

14. See Carl E. Braaten, "Christocentric Trinitarianism vs. Unitarian Theocentrism," *Journal of Ecumenical Studies* 24, no. 1 (Winter 1987).

15. See Thomas J. J. Altizer, Max A. Meyers, Carl A. Raschke, Robert P. Scharlemann, Mark C. Taylor, and Charles E. Winquist, *Deconstruction and Theology* (New York: Crossroad, 1982).

16. See Mark C. Taylor, *Erring: A Postmodern A-Theology* (Chicago: University of Chicago Press, 1987).

17. Langdon Gilkey, *Naming the Whirlwind: The Renewal of God Language* (Indianapolis: Bobbs-Merrill Co., 1969), 20. Frederick Ferré, *Language, Logic and God* (Chicago: University of Chicago Press, 1961), 160.

18. Sharon D. Welch, *Communities of Resistance and Solidarity: A Feminist Theology of Liberation* (Maryknoll, N.Y.: Orbis Books, 1985), 1, 2.

19. Ibid., 7.

20. See Carl E. Braaten and Robert W. Jenson, eds., *Christian Dogmatics,* 2 vols. (Philadelphia: Fortress Press, 1984).

21. Edwards quoted in Robert W. Jenson, *America's Theologian: A Recommendation of Jonathan Edwards* (New York: Oxford University Press, 1988), 18.

22. Ibid.

23. Sallie McFague, *Metaphorical Theology* (Philadelphia: Fortress Press, 1982), 1. See Simone Weil, *Waiting for God* (New York: Harper & Row, n.d.).

24. Ibid., 194.

25. See Sallie McFague, *Models of God: Theology for an Ecological, Nuclear Age* (Philadelphia: Fortress Press, 1987).

26. See Robert W. Jenson, *The Triune Identity* (Philadelphia: Fortress Press, 1982).

27. Knitter, *No Other Name?* 156.

28. Martin Luther, "Confession Concerning Christ's Supper," in *Martin Luther's Basic Theological Writings,* ed. Timothy F. Lull (Minneapolis: Fortress Press, 1989), 378.

Chapter 2: Absoluteness Is a Predicate of God's Kingdom

1. See H. G. Glockner, vol. 1 of his *Hegel-Lexikon,* in H. Glockner, ed., vols. 23–26 of *Hegel: Sämtliche Werke* (Stuttgart, 1927–39; distributed Adler's Foreign Books, Evanston, Ill.).

2. See Gotthold E. Lessing, *Nathan the Wise,* trans. Günther Reinhardt (Brooklyn: Barron's Educational Series, 1950).
3. Quoted by Karl Barth, *Protestant Theology in the Nineteenth Century* (Valley Forge: Judson Press, 1973), 253.
4. Karl Barth, vol. 4, part 1, of *Church Dogmatics,* trans. G. W. Bromiley (Edinburgh: T. & T. Clark, 1956), 386–87.
5. Karl Barth, *The Epistle to the Romans,* trans. Edwyn C. Hoskyns (New York: Oxford University Press, 1968), 204.
6. *Revolutionary Theology in the Making: Barth-Thurneysen Correspondence 1914-1925,* trans. James D. Smart (Richmond: John Knox, 1964), 36.
7. Ernst Benz, "Ideas for a Theology of the History of Religion," in *The Theology of the Christian Mission,* ed. Gerald H. Anderson (New York: McGraw-Hill, 1961), 135.
8. Wolfhart Pannenberg, "Toward a Theology of the History of Religions," in vol. 2 of *Basic Questions in Theology: Collected Essays* (Louisville, Ky.: Westminster John Knox, 1983), 65–118.
9. Wilfred Cantwell Smith, *Towards a World Theology* (Philadelphia: Westminster Press, 1981); John Hick, *God and the Universe of Faiths* (New York: Macmillan Co., 1963); John Cobb, *Beyond Dialogue* (Philadelphia: Fortress Press, 1982); Knitter, *No Other Name?*
10. Wolfhart Pannenberg, "The Basis of Ethics in the Thought of Ernst Troeltsch," in *Ethics,* trans. Keith Crim (Philadelphia: Westminster Press, 1981), 87.
11. Quoted by Gunnar v. Schlippe, *Die Absolutheit des Christentums bei Ernst Troeltsch auf dem Hintergrund der Denkfelder des 19. Jahrhunderts* (Neustadt an der Aisch: Verlag Degener & Co., 1966), 9.
12. Ernst Troeltsch, *The Absoluteness of Christianity and the History of Religions,* trans. David Reid (Richmond, Va.: John Knox Press, 1971), 45.
13. Ibid., 63.
14. Ibid., 79.
15. Ibid., 108.
16. John Hick, *God and the Universe of Faiths,* 131. See also his *The Myth of God Incarnate* (Philadelphia: Westminster Press, 1977).
17. Ernst Troeltsch, *Writings on Theology and Religions,* trans. Robert Morgan and Michael Pye (New York: Gerald Duckworth & Co., 1977), 189. 2d ed. (Louisville, Ky.: Westminster/John Knox, 1990).
18. John Hick, "Christ's Uniqueness," *Reform* (1974): 18.
19. Paul F. Knitter, "New Dialogue with Buddhism," *Horizons* 8, no. 1 (1981): 57.
20. Paul F. Knitter, "Jesus—Buddha—Krishna: Still Present?" *Journal of Ecumenical Studies* 16, no. 4 (Fall 1979): 659.
21. Karl Jaspers, *Philosophical Faith and Revelation* (London: Collins, 1967), 342.
22. Robert Morgan, "Troeltsch and Christian Theology," in *Ernst Troeltsch, Writings on Theology and Religion,* 212.
23. Ernst Troeltsch, *The Absoluteness of Christianity and the History of Religions,* 145.

Notes

24. Wolfhart Pannenberg, *Theology and the Philosophy of Science* (Philadelphia: Westminster Press, 1976), 109.
25. Ibid.
26. Ibid., 110.
27. Pannenberg, "The Basis of Ethics" (see n. 9), 106.
28. Troeltsch, *The Absoluteness of Christianity and the History of Religions*, 118.
29. Eberhard Jüngel, *God as the Mystery of the World*, trans. Darrel L. Guder (Grand Rapids, Mich.: William B. Eerdmans Publishing Co., 1983), viii.
30. Paul Tillich, *Biblical Religion and the Search for Ultimate Reality* (Chicago: University of Chicago Press, 1955), 85.
31. Jüngel, *God as the Mystery of the World*, xiii.
32. Ibid., xiv.
33. Ibid., 12.
34. Ibid., 13.
35. Ibid., 19.
36. Ibid., 20.
37. Martin Kähler, *Das Kreuz: Grund und Mass für die Christologie* (Gütersloh: C. Bertelsmann Verlag, 1911).
38. Jüngel, *God as the Mystery of the World*, 35.
39. Ibid., 40.
40. See Pannenberg's thoughts on the doctrine of the Trinity in "Die Subjectivität Gottes und die Trinitätslehre" and "Christologie und Theologie," in vol. 2 of *Grundfragen systematischer Theologie* (Göttingen: Vandenhoek & Ruprecht, 1980).
41. Robert W. Jenson, *The Triune Identity* (Philadelphia: Fortress Press, 1982), 136.

Chapter 3: Christ Is the Heart of the Church's Message

1. John Hick, *God Has Many Names* (Philadelphia: Westminster Press, 1980), 90.
2. Colm O'Grady, *The Church in Catholic Theology: Dialog with Karl Barth* (London: Geoffrey Chapman, 1969), 106.
3. Lucien Richards, *What Are They Saying about Christ and World Religions?* (New York: Paulist Press, 1981), 12.
4. John Leith, ed., *Creeds of the Churches*, 3d ed. (Atlanta: John Knox Press, 1983), 520.
5. Tom F. Driver, *Christ in a Changing World: Toward an Ethical Christology* (New York: Crossroad, 1981), 65.
6. Paul F. Knitter, "Towards a Theocentric/Nonnormative Christology: Growing Endorsement" (Paper given to the Currents in Contemporary Christology Group at the American Academy of Religion), 11.
7. Gustafson, *Ethics from a Theocentric Perspective.*

8. See Eberhard Jüngel, *The Doctrine of the Trinity: God's Being Is in Becoming* (Grand Rapids, Mich.: William B. Eerdmans Publishing Co., 1976); Jürgen Moltmann, *The Crucified God* (New York: Harper & Row, 1981); Jenson, *The Triune Identity;* and Wolfhart Pannenberg, *Systematische Theologie* (Göttingen: Vandenhoek & Ruprecht, 1988). See also Adolph Harnack, *History of Dogma,* trans. Neil Buchannan (Magnolia, Mass.: Peter Smith, n.d.).

9. Luther quoted in T. Tappert, trans., *The Book of Concord* (Philadelphia: Fortress Press, 1959), 598.

10. Barth, "Religion as Unbelief," vol. 2, part 2 of *Church Dogmatics,* par. 17.

11. Ibid., 299.

12. Barth, vol. 4, part 3, *Church Dogmatics,* 3.

13. Ibid., 89.

14. Ibid., 90.

15. Ibid., 91.

16. Ibid., 93.

17. Ibid., 92.

18. Ibid., 97.

19. Ibid.

20. Ibid., 114.

21. Ibid., 115.

22. Ibid., 118.

23. Ibid., 122.

24. Ibid., 478.

25. Ibid., 355–56.

26. Barth, vol. 2, part 2 of *Church Dogmatics,* 167.

27. Barth, vol. 4, part 1 of *Church Dogmatics,* 747.

Chapter 4: Christ is God's Final, Not the Only, Revelation

1. Symmachus quoted in Arnold Toynbee, *Christianity among the Religions of the World* (New York: Charles Scribner's Sons, 1957), 112.

2. Ibid.

3. Nicholas of Cusa quoted in Paul Tillich, *Christianity and the Encounter of the World Religions* (New York: Columbia University Press, 1977), 40–41.

4. John Hick, *God and the Universe of Faiths* (see chap. 2, n. 9). Hick calls for a "Copernican revolution" in our thinking about Christianity and the religions.

5. Paul Althaus, *The Theology of Martin Luther,* trans. Robert C. Schultz (Philadelphia: Fortress Press, 1966), 10–11.

6. See Barth, vol. 4, part 3 of *Church Dogmatics,* 114.

7. Ibid., 115.

8. See Knitter, *No Other Name?* 104.

9. Paul Althaus, "Die Inflation des Begriffs der Offenbarung in der gegenwärtigen Theologie," *Zeitschrift für systematische Theologie* 18 (1941): 143.

10. Ratschow quoted in Paul F. Knitter, *Towards a Protestant Theology of Religions* (Marburg: N. G. Elwert Verlag, 1974), 190. See also Carl Heinz Ratschow, *Die Religionen* (Gütersloh: Gütersloher Verlagshaus Gerd Mohn, 1979).

Notes

11. Ibid.
12. Wolfhart Pannenberg, *Jesus—God and Man,* trans. Lewis L. Wilkins and Duane A. Priebe (Philadelphia: Westminster Press, 1968), 130.
13. Ratschow quoted in Knitter, *Towards a Protestant Theology of Religions,* 190.
14. Raimundo Panikkar, "Salvation in Christ: Concreteness and Universality, The Supername" (Santa Barbara, Photocopy, 1972), 48.
15. Gustaf Wingren, *Credo: The Christian View of Faith and Life,* trans. Edgar M. Carlson (Minneapolis: Augsburg Publishing House, 1981), 183.

Chapter 5: Christianity Needs a Theology of Religions

1. Harvey Cox, *Many Mansions* (Boston: Beacon Press, 1988), 4.
2. Ibid., 5.
3. Ibid., 6.
4. Ibid., 8–9.
5. Albert Schweitzer, *The Quest for the Historical Jesus,* trans. W. Montgomery (London: Adam & Charles Black, 1910), 4.
6. See Jaroslav Pelikan, *Jesus through the Centuries* (New Haven: Yale University Press, 1985).
7. See J. Paul Rajashekar, ed., *Religious Pluralism and Lutheran Theology* (Geneva: Lutheran World Federation, 1988), report 23/24.
8. See Paul Varo Martinson, *A Theology of World Religions* (Minneapolis: Augsburg Publishing House, 1987).
9. Benz, "Ideas for a Theology of the History of Religion," 136.
10. Gandhi quoted by Hans Küng in *Christianity and World Religions,* trans. Peter Neinegg (Garden City, N.Y.: Doubleday & Co., 1986), 282.

Chapter 6: The Trinity Is the Model of the Church's Unity

1. The most important works on the Trinity by the named theologians are the following: Jüngel, *The Doctrine of the Trinity* and *God as the Mystery of the World;* Pannenberg, *Systematische Theologie;* Jürgen Moltmann, *The Trinity and the Kingdom,* trans. Margaret Kohl (San Francisco: Harper & Row, 1981); Walter Kasper, *The God of Jesus Christ,* trans. Matthew J. O'Connell (New York: Crossroad, 1984); Leonardo Boff, *Trinity and Society,* trans. Paul Burns (Maryknoll, N.Y.: Orbis Books, 1988); and Jenson, *The Triune Identity.*
2. Rahner, *The Trinity* (see introd., n. 6).
3. Ibid., 10–11.
4. Ibid., 14.
5. Ibid., 17.
6. See Johannes Feiner and Magnus Lohrer, eds., *Mysterium Salutis: Grundriss Heilsgeschichtlicher Dogmatik* (Eisiedeln: Benziger Verlag, 1967).
7. Barth, in vol. 2, part 2 of *Church Dogmatics,* 548.
8. Rahner, *The Trinity,* 17.
9. Kant quoted in Moltmann, *The Trinity and the Kingdom* (see n. 1), 6.

10. Friedrich Schleiermacher, *The Christian Faith* (Edinburgh: T. & T. Clark, 1928), 738.

11. Cyril C. Richardson, *The Doctrine of the Trinity* (New York: Abingdon Press, 1958), 15.

12. Section 3 of the Constitution of the World Council of Churches, 1.

13. Lesslie Newbigin, *Trinitarian Faith and Today's Mission* (Richmond, Va.: John Knox Press, 1963), 31.

14. Ibid., 13.

15. Ibid., 31.

16. Ibid., 9.

17. See Lesslie Newbigin, "The Enduring Validity of Cross Cultural Mission," *Together* (October–December 1988). This essay was based on a presentation at the Overseas Ministries Study Center in New Haven, Conn., October 1987.

18. Knitter, *No Other Name?* 145–46.

19. Ibid., 166.

20. Adolf von Harnack, *What Is Christianity?* trans. Thomas Baily Saunders (Philadelphia: Fortress Press, 1986), 144.

21. Hans Küng, "Toward an Ecumenical Theology of Religions," in *Christianity among World Religions: Concilium,* ed. Hans Küng and Jürgen Moltmann (Edinburgh: T. & T. Clark, 1986), 121–22.

22. Knitter, *No Other Name?* 165.

23. Moltmann, *The Trinity and the Kingdom,* 149.

24. Spinoza quoted in Jüngel, *God as the Mystery of the World,* 280.

25. Ibid., 309.

26. Wolfhart Pannenberg, "Problems of a Trinitarian Doctrine of God," *Dialog* 26 (Fall 1987): 256.

27. Cyprian quoted in Kasper, *The God of Jesus Christ* (see n. 1), 247.

28. Jenson, *The Triune Identity,* 29.

29. Ibid., 32.

30. Jürgen Moltmann, *The Church in the Power of the Spirit,* trans. Margaret Kohl (San Francisco, Harper & Row: 1977), 152.

Chapter 7: God the Creator Orders Public Life

1. See S. S. Maimela, comments in *God's Creative Activity through the Law* (Pretoria: The University of South Africa, 1984), 150 n. 6.

2. See Martin Heinecken, "Luther and 'the Orders of Creation' in Relation to the Doctrine of Work and Vocation," *The Lutheran Quarterly* 4 (November 1952): 396 n. 1.

3. See Adolf von Harless, "Schöpfungsordnungen," in *Die Religion in Geschichte und Gegenwart* (Tübingen: J. C. B. Mohr [Paul Siebeck], 1961), 1492–94.

4. See H. M. Kuitert's concept of the "empty world" in *Everything Is Politics but Politics Is Not Everything,* trans. John Bowden (Grand Rapids, Mich.: William B. Eerdmans Publishing Co., 1986), 77–87.

Notes

5. Karl Barth, vol. 3, part 4 of *Church Dogmatics* (Edinburgh: T. & T. Clark, 1961), 19–20.

6. This is the main point of Maimela's criticism of Werner Elert's theology; see *God's Creativity through the Law.*

7. Pannenberg, "On the Theology of Law," in *Ethics* (see chap. 2, n. 9), 27.

8. Helmut Thielicke, *Theological Ethics,* trans. John Doberstein (Philadelphia: Fortress Press, 1966), 439.

9. This was the case with Niels Hanson Söe, *Christliche Ethik* (Munich: Chr. Kaiser Verlag, 1949).

10. See Joseph Fletcher, *Situation Ethics: The New Morality* (Philadelphia: Westminster Press, 1966).

11. *Martin Luthers Werke, Kritische Gesamtausgabe* (Weimar, 1883–), I, 306ff.

12. *Martin Luthers Werke, Kritische Gesamtausgabe* (Weimar, 1883–), I, 311.

13. *Martin Luthers Werke, Kritische Gesamtausgabe* (Weimar, 1883–), XXVII, 418.

14. Paul Althaus, *Theologie der Ordnungen* (Gütersloh: C. Bertelsmann Verlag, 1935), 20.

15. See Gustaf Wingren, *Creation and Law,* trans. Ross Mackenzie (Philadelphia: Muhlenberg Press, 1958) and *Creation and Gospel* (New York: Edwin Mellen Press, 1979).

Index

Index

Weiss, Johannes, 41
Whitehead, A. N., 88
Wilkins, Lewis L., 140
Wingren, Gustaf, 67, 131,
140, 142
Winquist, Charles E., 18, 136
Wittgenstein, Ludwig, 19

Wright, G. Ernest, 16

Xavier, Francis, 72

Zizioulas, John, 107
Zoroaster, 40
Zwingli, Huldreich, 27, 53